Contents

Training Techniques 75

What's in the Food?
100

When Food = Poison
109

Grooming Must-Haves
115

Part Three—Plan for a Healthy Life 129

Vaccination Schedule 152

Other Pests and How to Treat Them 186–187

Dangerous Indoor & Outdoor Plants 226

Part One
A Healthy Start

"Tap Water! You bring me tap water? I ordered Root Beer!"

The Wide World Of Dogs

Welcome to the wide world of dogs! Maybe you already have a dog but are hoping to give your canine companion the best possible life. Maybe you are still waiting to bring a dog into your life but want to make sure you do everything right. Dogs and humans have lived together and depended upon each other for thousands of years, and we've learned a few things during all that history, not only about how to live more easily with an animal that was, after all, once completely wild, but also how to keep our canine friends happy, well-behaved, and in the best possible health.

This book is about making your dog's life–and by extension, your family's life–as healthy and happy as possible. It isn't enough to toss a handful of bargain

Dogs and people–perfect together!

Part 1

Dogs come in all shapes and sizes.

What's in a Name?

Many breeds are named after their function. Dachshund means "badger dog" in German, and the long, low Dachshund was originally bred to follow this fierce animal into its underground burrow. Labrador Retrievers were bred to retrieve ducks and possibly fish out of the field or water for hunters and fisherman. Scottish Deerhounds were bred for speed in order to chase down deer.

kibble in your dog's direction a couple of times a day. Keeping a dog healthy, well behaved, well adjusted, and a contributing family member takes some planning and some special knowledge, and that's what you'll find in these pages.

Just What Is a Dog?

Say the word "dog" and everyone knows what you mean: Man's best friend; buddy to your kids; a sympathetic ear; a head to pat; a friend to hug.

But what someone pictures when he or she hears the word "dog" is anyone's guess. Do you think of a dog as a Golden Retriever or a toy Poodle? A Rottweiler or a Shih Tzu?

Dogs are the most "plastic" of species. No other animal varies so much in size and appearance–not cats, beetles, monkeys, or even humans. If we didn't know better, it would be hard to believe that the tiny, quivering Chihuahua you can hold in the palm of your

Group Dynamics

The American Kennel Club and the United Kennel Club different slightly in the groups of dogs they recognize. The AKC recognizes seven different groups:

- Sporting Dogs
- Hounds
- Working Dogs
- Terriers
- Toys
- Non-Sporting Dogs
- Herding Dogs

The UKC recognizes eight groups:

- Companion Breeds
- Guardian Dogs
- Gun Dogs
- Herding Dogs
- Northern Breeds
- Scenthounds
- Sighthounds/Pariahs
- Terriers

Knowing your dog's special needs will help you give him the best care.

hand and the petite but feisty Yorkie sitting primly on a little sofa cushion are members of the same species as that gigantic, hairy Irish Wolfhound loping across the dog park or that huge furry Newfoundland pulling its hapless owner down the street.

Because dogs are so varied in size, coat type, lifespan, working ability, and temperament, it's no surprise that one person's Labrador Retriever is another person's worst nightmare, or that "small-dog people" and "large-dog people" can bicker endlessly about the relative merits of an Italian Greyhound vs. a Great Dane.

But knowing about your individual dog's type and breed is more than a matter of aesthetics. Different kinds of dogs have many different kinds of qualities, including different

Be Selective

It's always a good idea to visit your local animal shelter several times during your search process. Perhaps the dog that perfectly matches your specifications is waiting for you there. However, don't let yourself be swept away by a pair of big brown eyes. If that lonely dog peering at you longingly from the kennel is of a type that doesn't match your needs, wants, or specifications, chances are the match won't be made in heaven. Keep looking. That dog may be perfect for someone else, and sad as it may be, no one can save all the dogs at the animal shelter. You will be most helpful to a rescued dog if you wait for the one you know you'll be able to keep.

Internet Info

One of the best things about the Internet (in my opinion) is that it makes searching for dog breed information so easy. Unfortunately, however, many websites about dogs and dog breeds contain inaccurate, misleading, or even dangerous information. When searching for information about the dog breeds that fascinate you, stick to those websites published by established organizations with good reputations like the American Kennel Club (www.akc.org) and the United Kennel Club (www.ukc.com) as well as national breed clubs consisting of people devoted to a particular breed and working in that breed's best interest. Dog magazine websites for publications like *Dog Fancy* (www.dogfancy.com) and *Dog World* (www.dogworldmag.com) also contain solid information.

kinds of health issues. Small dogs generally have longer life spans than large dogs. Large dogs are more prone to hip dysplasia and bone density problems, while small dogs are notorious for having kneecaps that don't stay in place (called luxating patellas). White dogs or dogs with large areas of white like Dalmatians tend to have skin allergies and are sometimes prone to deafness.

Certain types of dogs, like terriers, or certain breeds of dog, like Doberman Pinschers, are prone to certain diseases, like von Willebrand's disease (a chronic bleeding disorder), bloat (a condition in which the stomach twists), or canine intervertebral disc disease (a spinal disorder). Knowing your dog's breed and the tendencies associated with that breed, as well as with your dog's coat type, color, and size, will give you a head start in designing a healthy life plan for your new best friend.

Besides health issues, knowing your dog's group and breed can help you give your pet the healthiest kinds of food, exercise, mental stimulation, toys, and general care. While your Maltese and your Saluki both need love and care, their particular temperaments and needs

Who to Believe?

When you start researching your breed of choice, you might find conflicting information from different sources that all seem reputable. That's because some dog breeds have certain issues associated with them. For example, one Border Collie breed club believes Border Collies should work as herding dogs and never be shown in dog shows, while another equally reputable Border Collie breed club believes that Border Collies can be shown in dog shows and still retain their working abilities. Both are good clubs, both have members who sincerely care about Border Collies, and both have a point. However, health and care information from dog and breed club sites is usually pretty reliable. On the other hand, personal homepages featuring certain breeds can be fun to read with good pictures and interesting links (and differing strong opinions, too), but they may not always contain accurate care information.

are not identical. Your Maltese would probably rather sit on your lap, while your Saluki probably prefers a luxurious cushion across the room where she can keep an eye on you. Your Maltese probably needs to eat more often during the day, and your Saluki needs more room to exercise.

The Breed for You

Long before most dog breeds were "officially" named, groups or types of dogs looked very different. Sporting dogs, like the Irish Setter, Brittany, and Golden Retriever, scarcely resemble sled dogs like the Siberian Husky, Alaskan Malamute, and Samoyed. Pit bulls don't look like Collies, who don't look much like Airedales and wiry Jack Russells that are made for barreling through the bracken after a rat. Guardian dogs, like the Rottweiler, Doberman Pinscher, Great Dane, and Mastiff, barely resemble their toy cousins, such as the Miniature Pinscher, Pekingese, and Cavalier King Charles Spaniel.

Today, breed clubs like the American Kennel Club (AKC) and the United Kennel Club (UKC) categorize dogs into groups according to their original purpose, although different clubs group and name dog types somewhat differently. Knowing the kind of dog you want can help you to narrow the field before deciding on a breed. Knowing you want a terrier or a sporting dog or a companion breed that fits in your lap can make a big difference in whether the dog you finally choose will grow into your family successfully.

Every group or type of dog has certain distinctive characteristics, both physical and temperamental. If you think you want a Labrador Retriever, it is best to know first that sporting dogs such as Labs are very active, strong, boisterous, friendly, and tractable (they like to do what you say), but have very high energy and exercise needs. If that doesn't fit your idea of the perfect pet, you might consider broadening your search to include other possibilities.

Guardian-Type Dogs:

- Anatolian Shepherd
- Bernese Mountain Dog
- Boxer
- Bullmastiff
- Doberman Pinscher
- Dogo Argentino
- Dogue de Bordeaux
- Giant Schnauzer
- Great Dane
- Great Pyrenees
- Greater Swiss Mountain Dog
- Kangal Dog
- Komondor
- Kuvasz
- Leonberger
- Maremma Sheepdog
- Mastiff
- Neapolitan Mastiff
- Newfoundland
- Rottweiler
- Saint Bernard
- Standard Schnauzer
- Tibetan Mastiff

Once you know the type of dog that will best fit into your lifestyle, you can narrow your search down to an individual breed or breed type. And again, knowing the group and breed of your pet is also particularly relevant when it comes to making health care decisions for your pet. Sporting dogs, working dogs, toy dogs, and terriers all have certain health problems to which they are predisposed. They also each have unique care needs and preventive health practices that work best for them.

In other words, know your group, know your breed, know your individual dog, and know yourself! That's the formula to ensuring a healthy future for your four-legged family member.

Guardians

Mastiff dogs were large, powerful, and muscular, and are known to have existed as far back as the ancient Romans, where they were probably used as guardians and war dogs. Many of the guardian breeds evolved from the mastiff types; think Rottweilers, Dobermans, Great Danes, and St. Bernards.

Guardian breeds are still used today for guarding, protection, and work in the military and in law enforcement, as well as for search and rescue. Many pet owners have guardian dogs that are devoted family members who have a strong instinct to protect the home and family. However, owners of guardian dogs must be assertive and able to control a large dog, not with violence but with firm, consistent enforcement of appropriate house rules and with plenty of early socialization. Guard dogs don't need to be trained to have a guardian instinct, but they do need to be trained to control that instinct and to interact appropriately with other animals and with humans.

Herders

Herding dogs are typically medium to large in size with thick or wooly coats to keep them warm as they worked outside all day. They were probably used even thousands of years ago to herd and sometimes to guard flocks of sheep and cattle. Herding dogs remain valuable working members of family farms today.

Because herding breeds usually retain their herding instinct, in the absence of a flock of sheep, they may try to herd children, the family cat, or a local flock of ducks. Herding breeds are serious working dogs with very high energy and great intelligence. These dogs must get lots of physical and mental activity or they are likely to get bored and destructive or run away. Because herding breeds were bred to think and problem-solve for themselves, human companions to dogs in this group must be smarter than the dog and able to provide their pets with the stimulation they require for a happy and contented life.

Herding Breeds:

Australian Cattle Dog	Canaan Dog
Australian Kelpie	Collie
Australian Shepherd	German Shepherd Dog
Bearded Collie	Giant Schnauzer
Beauceron	Old English Sheepdog
Belgian Malinois	Puli
Belgian Sheepdog	Shetland Sheepdog (aka Sheltie)
Belgian Tervuren	
Border Collie	Stumpy Tail Cattle Dog
Bouvier Des Flandres	Cardigan Welsh Corgi
Briard	Pembroke Welsh Corgi

Originally, all dogs were bred for a purpose.

Sporting Dogs

American Water Spaniel	Gordon Setter
Barbet	Irish Setter
Brittany	Irish Water Spaniel
Chesapeake Bay Retriever	Labrador Retriever
Clumber Spaniel	Nova Scotia Duck Tolling Retriever
Cocker Spaniel	Pointer
Curly-Coated Retriever	Portuguese Water Dog
English Cocker Spaniel	Spinone Italiano
English Pointer	Standard Poodle
English Setter	Sussex Spaniel
English Springer Spaniel	Vizsla
Field Spaniel	Weimeraner
Flat-Coated Retriever	Welsh Springer Spaniel
German Shorthaired Pointer	Wirehaired Pointing Griffon
German Wirehaired Pointer	
Golden Retriever	

Sporting Dogs

Sporting dogs were used to help humans hunt small game, first by helping lure game into traps, and eventually, with the advent of firearms, by pointing to small game or birds, stopping and sitting (to avoid getting in the line of fire), then retrieving the fallen game. Some dogs of this type probably spend much of their time as companions and helpers to fisherman, "herding" fish into nets and retrieving fish from the water.

The sporting group includes the pointers, retrievers, setters, spaniels, the Brittany, and some of the more all-purpose hunting dogs like Vizlas and Weimeraners. Once the sporting breeds became more specialized, pointers and setters were used to locate the game so the hunters could flush it out and shoot it. Spaniels hunted ahead of their humans to flush game out of the dense underbrush. Retrievers would gently retrieve the downed game. All the sporting breeds were bred to do their job, then sit or stand still to avoid getting in the way, unlike the hound breeds that more actively chase down game.

The sporting dogs evolved to hunt with humans, and today even those that don't work as hunting companions tend to bond closely with their people. The sporting breeds are usually tractable–easy to train and eager to please. They make active, friendly companions but need to be kept busy so they don't become destructive. Because most sporting breeds are larger than lap-dog size, they do require plenty of daily exercise.

Sighthounds/Scenthounds

The Hound Group consists of dogs that also evolved to help humans hunt, but in a different way than the sporting breeds. Hounds work out in front of the hunters, who may be on foot or on horseback, to get the game running. English foxhounds would run in packs to flush out foxes so their aristocratic masters could engage in a spirited chase. Bloodhounds, Beagles, and Basset Hounds have skin folds and droopy ears that retain scent, making them able to follow scent trails for miles. These breeds are often used in law enforcement to track down criminals or locate drugs or explosives (although other non-hound breeds often excel at these jobs, too). Many hunters, particularly in the southern US, continue to use hound dogs in the field today.

Versatility

Why are some breeds listed under more than one group? Some breeds are highly specialized, and others are quite versatile. For example, Giant Schnauzers and Standard Schnauzers both make excellent guardian dogs, but they also have an uncanny instinct for herding.

Popularity Contest

The Labrador Retriever has been the most popular dog in American Kennel Club registrations since 1991, with no indication that it will relinquish that top spot.

Every group has distinctive talents and characteristics.

Hounds

Scenthounds:	Sighthounds:
American Foxhound	Afghan Hound
Basset Hound	Basenji
Beagle	Borzoi
Black and Tan Coonhound	Carolina Dog
Black Mouth Cur	Greyhound
Bloodhound	Ibizan Hound
Bluetick Coonhound	Irish Wolfhound
Dachshund	Italian Greyhound
English Coonhound	New Guinea Singing Dog
English Foxhound	Pharaoh Hound
Harrier	Rhodesian Ridgeback
Leopard Cur	Saluki
Mountain Cur	Scottish Deerhound
Norwegian Elkhound	Whippet
Otterhound	
Petit Basset Griffon Vendeen	
Plott Hound	
Redbone Coonhound	
Treeing Cur	
Treeing Tennessee Brindle	
Treeing Walker Coonhound	

Over-Achievers

The towering Irish Wolfhound was largely responsible for the extinction of wolves in Ireland in the late 18th century. After the wolves were gone, the Wolfhound population soon dwindled to near extinction for lack of a job.

Sighthounds, sometimes called gaze-hounds, also have a keen sense of smell but were developed to hunt by sight. These dogs are among the most ancient breeds, according to archeological evidence. Many indigenous or native dogs, especially in hot climates like Africa, share characteristics with the sighthounds, and the art of ancient Egypt suggests that Greyhound-type dogs were common at the time.

In general, hounds tend to be less obedient than sporting dogs because they had to learn to hunt on their own, far from hearing range of the hunter. These independent thinkers are often proficient escape artists and will follow a scent or a small moving object with no thought to looking both ways before crossing a street, so human companions of hound breeds must be extra vigilant in keeping their friends safe (in other words, keep that leash on!).

Leader of the Pack

Sled dogs like Siberian Huskies and Alaskan Malamutes are fiercely hierarchical. They often squabble with other dogs competing for their place in the pack rank. To live peacefully with a sled dog, humans must be assertive and consistent so the dogs don't try to become leader of the pack. When everyone knows who ranks where, everyone is more likely to get along.

Spitz Dogs

- Akita
- Alaskan Klee Kai
- Alaskan Malamute
- American Eskimo
- Canadian Eskimo Dog
- Chinese Shar-Pei
- Chinook
- Chow Chow
- Finnish Spitz
- Kai
- Karelian Bear Dog
- Keeshond
- Lundehund
- Norwegian Elkhound
- Samoyed
- Shiba Inu
- Siberian Husky

Spitzes

Spitz-type dogs look very similar to wolves and have served as all-purpose dogs, able to hunt, herd, and pull sleds and carts for centuries. Nordic spitz types like the Alaskan Malamute and Siberian Husky were integral to arctic cultures, and Asian spitz types like Chow Chows and Akitas probably served as family guardians and working dogs in rural areas. Most arctic areas in the world have a native spitz-type dog, from Alaska to Finland to Russia to the Arctic Circle.

Spitz dogs can be challenging. They are highly intelligent and bond closely with their owners, but tend to be indifferent to, if not suspicious of, strangers. They have a strong protective instinct and unlike a louder, more obvious guard dog, spitzes are stealthy and quiet in their approach—meter readers and mail people beware.

Spitzes were bred to work hard. Siberian Huskies, Alaskan Malamutes, and other sled dog types have enough energy to pull your whole family on a sled, probably into the next county. All that energy must be channeled with plenty of exercise and doggy activities like sledding, skijoring (pulling a person on cross-country skis), weight pulling, or hiking if you want your spitz to calm down when he is in the house. A spitz breed without anything to do is likely to get destructive or try to escape.

Keep your spitz busy with lots of exercise and plenty of daily human interaction. Socialize your spitz puppy to all kinds of people and dogs, and you'll have a happy, well-adjusted canine companion. While spitz types tend to be hearty and weather-resistant, and while they love the cold, they won't be happy outside all alone day in and day out, and they are not typically heat-tolerant. They need to stay cool, and they require human interaction.

Terriers

The terriers are native to the British Isles, where farms often had to contend with vermin and where poorer farmers, unable to keep specialized sporting breeds and hounds for hunting, needed small, all-purpose dogs to help tree squirrels and chase down rabbits and other small game. According to some accounts, small terriers were perfect for poaching because they could quickly hide in the farmer's coat at the approach of the rich landowner.

Bred to be small and extra feisty, many terriers have smooth or wiry coats that are perfect for barreling though the bracken after rats, badgers, rabbits, and foxes. Sometimes used on the hunt even today, terriers could tree a squirrel as easily as they could de-rat a granary. A terrier will bark ferociously to pinpoint an animal in its underground burrow, and will probably be happy to burrow in after it in the same way it will burrow under your covers at night (and most terriers are good at convincing their humans that such a practice is perfectly acceptable).

Any human companion to a terrier must be firm, consistent, and patient. Terriers can be obstinate and have minds of their own. They may not like your rules and will continually test their limits, attempting to re-establish their own tiny little autocracy. If you hate barking, consider another breed. While terriers can be trained to tone it down, barking is a part of this group and was an essential skill for their original purpose. No terrier is going to be quiet all the time.

Beneath Terra Firma

"Terrier" is from the Latin word for *terra*, which means "earth," because terriers were bred to follow small animals into their underground burrows or dig them out of their tunnels. Many terriers today still love to dig, and are notorious for wiggling under the bedcovers at night.

Terriers

Airedale Terrier	Irish Terrier	Silky Terrier
American Pit Bull Terrier	Jack Russell Terrier	Skye Terrier
American Staffordshire Terrier	Kerry Blue Terrier	Smooth Fox Terrier
	Lakeland Terrier	Soft Coated Wheaten Terrier
Australian Terrier	Manchester Terrier	Staffordshire Bull Terrier
Bedlington Terrier	Miniature Bull Terrier	Teddy Roosevelt Terrier
Border Terrier	Miniature Schnauzer	Toy Fox Terrier
Bull Terrier	Norfolk Terrier	Treeing Feist
Cairn Terrier	Norwich Terrier	Welsh Terrier
Cesky Terrier	Rat Terrier	West Highland White Terrier
Dandie Dinmont Terrier	Scottish Terrier	Wire Fox Terrier
German Pinscher	Sealyham Terrier	

Companion Dogs

While a two-pound dog probably wouldn't evolve in nature on its own, humans have been cultivating and refining toy dogs for thousands of years. Popular among European and Asian royalty in past centuries, companion breeds were bred to provide their bored and palace-bound masters with affection, warmth, and entertainment. Many of the smallest breeds come from Asia, where miniaturization has long been an art form: the Pekingese, Shih Tzu, and Pug are a few examples. Other toy dogs were designed to look like larger dogs but in miniature form. The Pomeranian is a miniature-sized spitz breed. The toy spaniels like the Cavalier King Charles Spaniel, are small and snuggly versions of sporting dogs. The Italian Greyhound is a

Small dogs can make great companions.

Toy Problems

Some toy breeds are prone to collapsing tracheas, causing them to cough or gag when they eat or drink. Severe cases can make breathing more difficult, and toy dogs may tire more easily. Collapsing tracheas occur most often in adult dogs, but puppies are occasionally affected.

TOYS

Affenpinscher	Lhasa Apso
Bichon Frise	Lowchen
Bolognese	Maltese
Boston Terrier	Miniature Pinscher
Brussels Griffon	Papillion
Cavalier King Charles Spaniel	Pekingese
	Pomeranian
Chihuahua	Pug
Chinese Crested	Schipperke
English Toy Spaniel	Shih Tzu
French Bulldog	Tibetan Spaniel
Havanese	Tibetan Terrier
Italian Greyhound	Poodle—Miniature and Toy
Japanese Chin	Yorkshire Terrier

sighthound in miniature, and the Yorkshire Terrier is a feisty, fiery terrier with a lap dog's tiny size and luxurious coat.

Toy dogs are small and delicate, so they aren't ideal companions for small children because they could be injured. Some toys feel competitive with children, but if given lots of indulgent attention, can be perfectly happy in a family with gentle older children who know how to handle them. Although your toy dog may be cute, don't spoil her! These tiny dogs can become miniature dictators.

Many toy dogs are overweight from too many treats and very badly behaved because they are constantly overindulged and not required to follow the house rules. Cute and small they may be, but they can also be yappy, aggressive, and destructive. Well-trained, well-socialized toy dogs make excellent companions, particularly for singles, small families, seniors, and the housebound. Because they are so small, they can get most of the exercise they need scampering around indoors.

Bad to the Bone?

The pit bull—a name often assigned to a group of dogs, including the American Pit Bull Terrier, the American Staffordshire Terrier, and the Staffordshire Bull Terrier—has a shady reputation, but this affectionate, devoted breed adores children and makes an excellent family pet when treated well and socialized properly.

Big Dog, Tiny Package

The Chihuahua is the smallest of all dog breeds, although certain Chihuahuas may be larger than certain members of other toy breeds, such as Toy Poodles and Yorkshire Terriers. Most Chihuahuas weigh less than six pounds, and some weigh barely two pounds.

Pick Your Breed

Once you've got an idea of the kind of dog you want, you can have a lot of fun perusing the different breed possibilities. The American Kennel Club (AKC) ranks dog breeds by popularity (according to how many dogs of each breed are registered with their organization each year). Below are the AKC's 50 most popular dogs (their most recent list as of press time), with brief descriptions of the top ten.

Of course, that doesn't mean you *have* to have one of the most popular dogs. An Italian Greyhound (#51), a Dalmatian (#58), a Jack Russell Terrier (#70), an American Eskimo Dog (#104), an Affenpinscher (#118), or a Sussex Spaniel (#148) might just be your perfect match.

Many rare breeds, including breeds not recognized by the AKC make fascinating and wonderful pets, as long as you do your research and are prepared for your dog's special needs and qualities. And don't forget

Pick the right breed for you and your family.

mixed breed dogs! Many mixed breeds are waiting in animal shelters for the perfect human match, and the animal shelter is a great place to look for a new best friend.

Of course, these breeds are popular for a good reason: They make great companions for the right people with the right kinds of lifestyles. Just remember to research your breed carefully before you buy.

The Ten Most Popular Dogs
*according to the American Kennel Club

1. Labrador Retriever

This native of Newfoundland (not Labrador) is the most popular dog in America. A medium-sized sporting breed with an agreeable personality and lots of energy, the Lab makes a great pet for active people who plan to spend a lot of time with their pet.

2. Golden Retriever

The second most popular dog in America is another sporting dog of similar size to the Lab, but with a longer, wavy golden coat. This native of the Scottish highlands is also active, sensitive, and requires lots of love.

3. German Shepherd Dog

This herding breed is more often used as a police, military, search-and-rescue, and assistance dog. Highly intelligent with a strong protective instinct, this German breed has been popular since the days of Rin Tin Tin, but requires an assertive and interactive human companion.

4. Dachshund

Known affectionately as the "wiener dog," this German hound was originally designed to follow badgers into their dens. The Dachshund comes in two sizes–standard and miniature–and three coat types–smooth, longhaired, and wirehaired, but all Dachshunds love to cuddle with, amuse, and joyfully defy their humans.

Sporting dogs, like Golden Retrievers, are very popular.

5. Beagle

Everybody loves a Snoopy dog, but Beagles, while affectionate and playful, will follow a scent across traffic or miles away from home. Ruled by their noses and notorious for their barks and baying, this British descendent of the Foxhound remains a capable hunter and tracker, as well as a jolly and affectionate family pet.

6. Yorkshire Terrier

This terrier may be tiny, but don't underestimate the Yorkie's watchdog abilities, vermin hunting skills, or air of self-importance. This British breed has a high maintenance coat and is easy to spoil, but a well-trained Yorkie who gets plenty of human companionship will make a delightful and devoted family member.

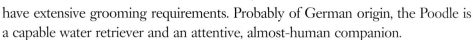

The Boxer is a loving addition to any household.

7. Poodle

The highly intelligent, personable, non-shedding Poodle comes in three varieties. The toy, miniature, and standard are all considered one breed, and all have extensive grooming requirements. Probably of German origin, the Poodle is a capable water retriever and an attentive, almost-human companion.

8. Boxer

This strong, powerful German breed was created to be a versatile working, guard, and companion dog. Boxers are easy to train and thrive when their lifestyles are active and their activities include their people.

9. Chihuahua

This tiny Mexican dog may fit in your coffee cup, but with his feisty, terrier-like attitude, he's ready to take on any dog, no matter how big. Chihuahua owners must be patient, consistent, vigilant about this small dog's safety, and able to avoid spoiling this potentially Napoleonic tyrant.

Part 1

Dogs with long coats, like the Shih Tzu, need regular grooming.

10. Shih Tzu

The Shih Tzu originated in China, descended from the older Lhasa Apso from Tibet. This longhaired small breed is heavy for its size, tough to groom, and decidedly mischievous but agreeable with other pets and a master at the game of human companionship.

Whatever breed you choose, as long as you are prepared for the particular qualities of your dog and make the commitment to socialize, train, and keep your dog in good health, you and your new pet can have a long and successful relationship together.

Wondering About the Rest?

Below are the rest of the top 50 most popular breeds of dog in the US:

11. Rottweiler	24. Doberman Pinscher	38. Chinese Shar-Pei
12. Pomeranian	25. Bichon Frise	39. Akita
13. Miniature Schnauzer	26. Pembroke Welsh Corgi	40. Papillion
14. Cocker Spaniel	27. English Springer Spaniel	41. Chesapeake Bay Retriever
15. Pug	28. Great Dane	42. Cairn Terrier
16. Shetland Sheepdog (aka Sheltie)	29. Weimeraner	43. Scottish Terrier
17. Miniature Pinscher	30. West Highland White Terrier	44. Cavalier King Charles Spaniel
18. Boston Terrier	31. Brittany	45. Vizsla
19. Bulldog	32. Pekingese	46. Airedale Terrier
20. Maltese	33. Collie	47. Great Pyrenees
21. Siberian Husky	34. Lhasa Apso	48. Bloodhound
22. German Shorthaired Pointer	35. Australian Shepherd	49. Bullmastiff
23. Basset Hound	36. Saint Bernard	50. Newfoundland
	37. Mastiff	

*This list is the most current list available from the American Kennel Club as of press time. The 50 most popular dog lists changes slightly each year and the most current list can be found on the American Kennel Club's website at www.akc.org/breeds under "Registration Statistics."

Thinking Like a Dog

Your German Shepherd looks like she's thinking about something. Her gaze is intense as she stares out the window. What does she see? What has captured her interest? She turns to look at you, and you wonder what she could possibly be thinking. Do dogs think? Do dogs feel? What is going through that canine brain?

Scientists, particularly animal behaviorists, have speculated on the thought process of the dog for centuries. Dogs came from wolves, right? So doesn't it follow that knowing how wolves behave and treating your dog accordingly is the secret to communicating with your dog? Dogs must want to move in packs, howl at the moon, and chase game, right?

Dogs have evolved through centuries of breeding and domestication.

Our pets depend on us to take care of their needs.

Each dog has his own individual personality.

Yes and no.

Dogs did evolve from wolves thousands of years ago, but the two species have been evolving separately for so long that they have distinctly different behaviors. While dogs and wolves have certain things in common, they have many important differences, too. Some dogs tend to enjoy hanging around with other dogs, but some much prefer to be the sole pampered pet in a household of humans. Some dogs bay at the moon, but some have no interest in such uncivilized behavior. Some dogs have a high prey drive and like to chase anything that moves, but that doesn't mean they will catch it, or know what to do with it if they do catch it, and some dogs don't even notice that squirrel on the lawn. A well-fed dog doesn't need to hunt and would probably rather share your cheeseburger, thank you very much. Then again, other dogs still retain that instinct to chase.

So how do you know what your German Shepherd is thinking? Does she have an eye on that cat across the street? The flock of grackles in the Sycamore tree? The neighbor mowing his lawn? Does she want to play, beg, chase, fight, or herd those baby ducks in the pond at the park?

Knowing how your dog thinks is just part of a puzzle that you, your dog's companion, get to put together, piece by piece. Your dog's breed is certainly part of the answer. A herding dog is more likely to be focused on his job and on your direction, whether the job is herding sheep or running an agility obstacle course. A toy dog is probably more focused on getting your attention and scoring a comfy spot on the nicest piece of furniture in the house. Because your dog is built a certain way and has evolved a certain way, he doesn't think or feel like a human. His physical and psychological needs are different.

Personality Puzzle

Like people, dogs have their own, individual personalities. While many Border Collies have a strong herding instinct and are intensely focused on their task, some defy the rules and prefer the couch. While some Doberman Pinschers have a strong protective instinct, a few individuals will be happy to lead the nice burglar to the family silver. Knowing a breed's tendencies is helpful in determining what your pet will be like and what his tendencies will be, but you'll never be able to predict any dog's personality completely. You have to get to know them. Then again, that's the fun part of living with a dog!

Through domestication, dogs have become our guardians and partners.

From Wolf to Pariah to Pet?

Once upon a time, there were no domestic dogs, or what scientists call *canis familiarus*. There were wolves, coyotes, and jackals, but no dogs. Many have speculated about how dogs "appeared," but most scientists agree that tamer wolves probably started hanging around humans because of the food humans discarded. Eventually, those canines that became helpful to humans, by protecting, guarding, and assisting on the hunt, were fed the most and probably survived the longest, reproducing more of their own kind. The domestic dog, in other words, probably evolved out of a joint evolutionary process–part survival instinct, part selection by humans.

Some dogs evolved to live near human settlements and live off human garbage. These "pariah" dogs exist today in many countries around the world. They aren't tame, exactly, but they know where the food is, and they don't tend to be aggressive. These pariah dogs look similar all over the world, suggesting that a certain physical structure is most beneficial, in evolutionary terms, to the scavenging life. Pariah dogs tend to be medium in size with short- to medium-length coats (often speckled), pointed ears, dropped but slightly curving tails, long legs, and an instinct to stay close–but not too close–to humans.

We have trained our dogs to work with us in many endeavors.

Wolves-n-Wildlife

According to Wolves-n-Wildlife, a California-based educational facility dedicated to wildlife preservation, there are only 3,200 to 3,500 wolves in the lower 48 states. Alaska is home to 5,000-6,000 wolves, and up to 60,000 wolves live in Canada. Check out more facts about wolves at the Wolves-n-Wildlife website, at http://www.wolvesnwildlife.org/.

Meanwhile, those dogs that humans took on as helpers and companions evolved into all kinds of different forms, from tiny Chihuahua to towering Great Dane. Today, wolves, pariah dogs, and pet dogs all share the same earth, but have their separate niches. They all have similarities, but they are not the same. Wolves live in the wild. Pariah dogs live on the fringes of human society. And, as you well know, pet dogs live with us. Sometimes, they even sleep under the quilts in the crooks of our knees or warming our feet. (Admit it!)

We know domestic dogs are different from wolves in many ways. For example, wolves are extremely difficult to tame. While it can be done, tame wolves are not like tame dogs. They are more fearful, less predictable, and more prone to attack when cornered. Wolves and wolf hybrids can be submissive, even cowering. They may bite out of fear. They can also be friendly and playful. But you can never be as sure of what to expect as you can with a domestic dog. Wolves are more likely to rely only on themselves for their survival, and if let loose, they are likely to run away. They might come back, or they might not.

Sure, some dogs do those things, especially when they haven't been well socialized and trained. However, a puppy that is socialized to many different people, trained well, and given lots of human attention is a much more predictable, dependable, and safe animal to have around than a "tamed" wolf, no matter what the breed. Wolves are amazing, fascinating, beautiful creatures, but they haven't evolved to be pets.

Dogs have evolved for so many centuries to live with humans that they have adapted in ways that make them appropriate and happy companions. When compared to a wild animal, dogs are easy to live with. In many cases, dogs are even essential for human livelihood, whether that means working as a farm hand, hunting hound, or companion.

Yet, they are still animals. They don't speak English (although many dogs can learn to understand a large number of words). They don't know (until we teach them) that they aren't supposed to relieve themselves in the house, scratch the furniture, chew your shoes, play tug of war with the curtains, play-bite human fingers, or bark hysterically at the dog on the other side of the fence.

Socialization is important for a well-adjusted, happy puppy.

Dogs are happy, even eager, to learn the rules. They want to please us, they enjoy doing what makes their people happy, and they live for praise, attention, affection, and of course, a nice treat. Dogs will joyfully spin in circles, sit, lie down, shake, play dead, pull a wheelchair, pick up a remote control, fetch a newspaper, or lick away tears. Dogs are made for us as we (one could easily argue) were made for dogs.

In their relatively short evolution into human companion, dogs have also evolved physically into a unique creature, wildly varied in morphology but with some common traits. Knowing how a dog is built is key to knowing how to keep a dog healthy, so let's look at the body of a dog, and what it says about dog health and even dog behavior.

Dogs are happy and eager to learn the rules and please their master.

Your dog sees the world from a different perspective.

The Body of the Dog

Obviously, dogs are built differently than humans. Dogs walk on four legs instead of two. They have tails and muzzles, fur and paws. They have a different perspective on the world. Some of them have eyes less than a foot off the ground.

Think about how the world appears from a dog's perspective. People must look like strange, towering creatures, surprisingly stable on their two legs, hardly victims waiting to be attacked but possibly foes to be feared, unless they prove themselves benevolent. Children must seem unpredictable, kinetic, somewhat like peers and yet, strangely different with their groping hands. And who knows how your own individual pet will interpret the behavior of all the many other creatures it may encounter during a lifetime: cats, guinea pigs, parakeets, squirrels, crows, strangers, intruders, neighbors, friends, and lots and lots of other dogs, some aggressive, some friendly, some indifferent, some instant canine buddies.

A dog has an amazing sense of sight, smell, and hearing.

Dogs, Not People

It's easy to assume that dogs think like us, and perhaps they do in some ways, but their unusual vantage, their increased senses, their different physical structure, and their limited (but not *that* limited) intelligence make a dog's perspective much different than a human's perspective. Assigning human characteristics to an animal (or to anything else that isn't human) is called *anthropomorphism*.

Even though your Rottweiler might toss toys into the air with his front paws, dogs don't have hands and don't begin to approach a human's manual dexterity. All four paws are primarily for walking, but as puppies, dogs use their mouths in much the same way humans use their hands–to explore their environments. Your terrier can hear sounds in the night you'll never hear. Your Beagle can smell so much better than you can that she can detect thousands of different smells, can follow a human trail for miles, can even detect cancer cells in skin samples and the chemical changes preceding a seizure in the humans around her.

Your Afghan can see a rabbit rustling in the underbrush from miles away and can get there faster than you could on a bicycle. Dogs are very fast. Just try to get a hold of that tiny Yorkshire Terrier if he doesn't want to let you, let alone outrun a Greyhound! These keen senses and high speed, along with strong jaws and sharp teeth, have helped dogs to survive. Dogs can sense danger, run away quickly, or fight if they must. They are also experts at finding food.

But the same traits that make dogs so adaptable also make them vulnerable to certain health conditions. Genetic diseases occur seemingly randomly in mixed breed dogs but occur in more obvious patterns in purebred dogs. When breeders isolate a gene pool of say, St. Bernards, certain genetic conditions and conditions related to physiology are likely to become more concentrated, so while mixed breeds get most genetic diseases, purebreds get more of just a few. For example, the strong bodies and deep chests of working dogs make them more prone to bloat, a dangerous and often fatal disease in which the stomach twists on itself. Dogs made to be long and low like Dachshunds and Pekingese are more likely to experience degenerative spinal disks resulting in canine intervertebral disk disease, another dangerous condition that can cause permanent paralysis.

The body structure of your dog may contribute to certain conditions.

Once again, you can see how knowing your individual pet's characteristics can help you to be

Your Fast Friend

Greyhounds can run faster than any other breed of dog. At full speed, a Greyhound can run about 45 miles per hour.

on the lookout for certain health conditions. Let's look at a dog's body piece by piece and talk about how different shapes, types, colors, and conditions predispose your dog to certain strengths and, inevitably, certain weaknesses.

What Your Dog's Anatomy Tells You

Dogs have legs, eyes, ears, backbones, hips, ribs, a heart, a liver, and many of the same organs and structures humans have. But they also have stifles, hocks, muzzles, pasterns, withers, and paws. See the drawing below to identify just what's what on your canine friend.

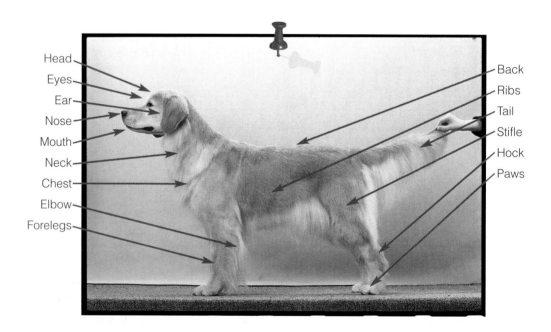

Knowing something about your dog's anatomy can help you know a lot about your dog's health and potential health issues. The kind of head, face, ears, coat, body shape, height, and even color can specifically impact your dog's needs, health risks, and care requirements. Let's look at what each part of your dog can tell you about her.

Body Talk

The *stop* is the part of a dog's face that separates the skull from the muzzle. Some dogs, like Golden Retrievers and Cocker Spaniels, have a well-defined stop. It's obvious where the skull ends and the muzzle starts. Others, like Greyhounds and Fox Terriers, have only a slight stop. These dogs have more wedge-shaped heads and the skull flows in almost a straight line into the muzzle. An American Staffordshire Terrier has a distinct stop, while a Bull Terrier has no stop at all.

Brachycephalic dogs, like the Boston Terrier, may have breathing problems.

Your Dog's Head and Face

First take a look at your dog's head and face. Some dogs have long, thin heads and muzzles, like a Whippet. Some have short, flat faces with barely a muzzle to be found, like a Pug or a Bulldog. Some dogs fall somewhere in the middle.

The flatness of your dog's face affects how well he breathes, sees, smells, and tastes. Dogs with very flat faces, called *brachycephalic* dogs, often snore, snort, and snuffle through life. Because their nasal passages are shortened, they are less tolerant of the heat and will be more susceptible to heat stroke. Brachycephalic airway syndrome is a more serious condition in which the shortened airway passages cause the dog to experience reduced oxygen intake. This condition's symptoms include blue-tinged skin, exercise intolerance, and severe snorting, snuffling, choking, gagging, open-mouthed breathing, and other sounds that suggest difficulty breathing. Other anatomical features that contribute to this condition in brachycephalic dogs are an elongated soft palate (this condition is largely responsible for that persistent snore emanating from your snoozing Pug) and nostrils that are pushed closed due to the flat face shape.

Brachycephalic dogs also tend to have large eyes that can be more vulnerable to injury. Skin folds can rub against the eyes causing irritation. Some dogs with large eyes have eyelids that don't completely close over their eyes, a condition that can result in blindness. They may also be prone to dry eyes. Your vet can prescribe an ointment for this problem. Eyeball prolapse is another emergency condition in which the dog's eyeball pops out. (If this happens, rush your pet and his eye to the emergency veterinary clinic immediately.)

If your dog has a flat face, make sure she stays cool in the summer. Never leave her in a parked car! Temperatures that would only mildly annoy a Labrador Retriever could spell disaster for a heavily coated, flat-faced Pekingese (although we strongly advise never leaving any dog in a parked car in warm weather). While some snoring and snorting is typical of a flat-faced breed, make sure to mention it to your veterinarian so he or she can continue to monitor your friend for problems. And watch out for those eyes! Teach children never to touch a dog's eyes.

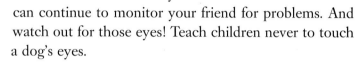

Make sure your dog's eyes are clear and free from irritation.

Some dogs get cataracts, usually in their senior years, but sometimes even as puppies. If your dog's eyes look cloudy, have her checked. Also see your vet if your dog's eyes look red or irritated. Dogs can get things in their eyes just like people. Some dogs are also prone to a genetic condition called entropion in which the eyelid grows in toward the eye, and eyelash hairs irritate the cornea.

Many breeds are also prone to progressive retinal atrophy or PRA. If your aging dog doesn't seem to see as well as he used to, have your vet check his eyes. PRA causes blindness, but a blind dog can still live comfortably and happily with his family with a little extra care. Less serious is the tear staining that occurs in some breeds. This staining is more noticeable in breeds with light coats. White Poodles, Bichons, and light-colored Pekingese often have tearstains, which is usually just a cosmetic problem. Ask your vet about products to treat it if it bothers you.

Dalmatian Sensation
The Dalmatian's original function was to run in front of horse-drawn fire engines to clear the way. They were the original fire sirens.

Dogs with white in their coats, like Beagles, can be prone to deafness.

Your Dog's Ears

A Basenji has short pointed ears. A Basset Hound has long droopy ears. A Fox Terrier has ears neatly folded over. What's the difference?

A dog's ear shape is more than a matter of looks. Dogs with long droopy ears are prone to skin infections in the folds of the ear, and dogs with very short ears are prone to ear infections, too, because the inner ear is less protected. Keep an eye on your dog's ears and call your vet if your dog starts to scratch his ears more often. Scratching could mean an infection or a pest infestation. Your vet should check your pet's ears at every annual check-up.

Dogs with large areas of white like Dalmatians and Beagles are prone to genetic deafness in one or both ears. Deaf dogs should never be bred, but they can make fine pets if you are prepared to make allowances for your dog's disability. However, if you don't know your dog is deaf, you can't meet her special needs. If you have a dog with a large amount of white on her coat or you have a senior dog that doesn't seem to hear you when you aren't making eye contact, ask your vet about testing your dog's hearing. If you bought your dog from a breeder, ask if the breeder did hearing tests on your dog. These are called BAER (brainstem auditory evoked response) tests, and they are the same tests they use on infants and small children.

The condition of a dog's coat is indicative of his overall health.

Doggy Dreadlocks

Some breeds have hair that easily works itself into dreadlock-type cords. The Puli and the Komondor grow beautifully corded coats. Poodle coats can also be worked into cords, although most people keep their poodles in a puppy cut, pet cut, or show cut.

Your Dog's Coat

Your dog's coat is an important health indicator. Whether he is a shaggy Bearded Collie or a sleek, shiny Doberman, a dog's coat can reveal the condition of his skin as well as his general health. Your dog's coat should be healthy and shiny. Bare patches can indicate skin allergies, skin infections, or parasites. A dull, sparse coat can also indicate a poor diet or other health problems. Let your vet know about any changes in your dog's coat.

Later in this book, you'll read about the importance of regular grooming sessions for monitoring your dog's health. Keeping your dog well groomed is also important for good health. Some dogs have wiry coats that require stripping to stay in good shape. Stripping involves plucking dead hairs from your dog's coat with your fingers or grooming tools designed for that purpose. Some dogs have long coats, curly coats, and/or double coats that require frequent attention to prevent them from matting. Mats in your dog's coat are difficult to remove and can attract dirt and pests because they make it difficult to get down to the skin when brushing and washing. Mats usually must be cut out of the dog's fur or shaved. Some people choose to keep their long-coated dogs cropped close to avoid mats, but those who want to keep their Pekingese, Poodle, or Puli in a show coat should be prepared for a lot of attention to grooming.

Your Dog's Body

The shape of your dog's body determines how she will move as well as what kind of health problems she might eventually have to face. Some dogs, like Great Danes and German Shepherds, have deep chests. Some dogs, like Pekingese and Skye Terriers, have long backs. Some dogs, like Dachshunds and Basset Hounds, have both.

Large dogs with deep chests are more prone to a severe health condition called bloat, also known as canine gastric dilation-volvulus (CGDV) or stomach torsion. This serious, life-threatening condition often results when large dogs are fed only once a day and gulp their food too quickly, sometimes followed by drinking a large amount of water and immediate vigorous exercise. When bloat occurs, the stomach twists and without immediate medical attention, the condition is usually fatal. Some dogs prone to bloat will experience it multiple times. For this reason, as a precaution especially in breeds prone to bloat, large and barrel-chested dogs should be fed smaller amounts more often–two to three meals a day instead of one–and encouraged to relax for approximately two hours after eating. In some breeds or bloodlines where bloat is a recurrent problem, gastroplexy may save an animal's life. This procedure anchors the stomach in any of several different ways, to prevent recurrence. Bloat is an emergency, and you have no time to wait. If you suspect your dog is experiencing bloat, take him to the vet or emergency pet care center immediately.

Do what you can to ensure your dog has a long, comfortable life.

Dogs who are longer than they are tall are prone to a different but also very serious condition called canine intervertebral disk disease or canine degenerative disk disease. This degenerative spinal condition can result in rupture of a spinal disk, and also occurs in humans. Because long-backed dogs have more pressure and movement on their spines than dogs with short backs and longer legs, the condition is more common in small dogs like Dachshunds and Pekingese. If not treated

Pick the diet, grooming routine, and exercise regimen that is right for your breed.

Bloat Alert

Some of the breeds more likely to be affected by bloat are the Akita, Bloodhound, Doberman Pinscher, Great Dane, Greyhound, German Shepherd, St. Bernard, Irish Wolfhound, Irish Setter, Weimeraner, and any large mixed breed with a deep chest. Although not tall dogs, Dachshunds and Basset Hounds are essentially medium-sized dogs with short legs, and can also be affected by bloat.

A giant breed like the Great Dane needs special care.

immediately, a disk rupture can result in permanent paralysis, so don't ignore stumbling, wobbling, yelps of pain when you touch your dog's back, or sudden refusals to move. Call your vet immediately.

Your Dog's Height

Your leggy, soon-to-be-towering Great Dane puppy and other large and giant breeds may be intimidating on the end of a leash, and they may be big goofy clowns at home, but growth like that comes with a few challenges. Large and giant breeds end up with a lot of bone. If a puppy grows too fast, his skeleton won't develop as well as it would at a slower growth rate, making your big baby susceptible to bone, joint, and cartilage disorders. Rather than feeding your large or giant breed a regular puppy food in his first year, which can be too high in protein and can result in too-rapid growth, feed a premium adult food or a puppy food specially formulated for large or giant breeds. Also feed appropriate amounts of food so your puppy grows at an appropriate rate and doesn't become overweight. Sure, it's impressive to see a little Mastiff puppy inhaling a huge volume of kibble, but it isn't healthy for him. Stick the to the amount of food your vet recommends, and a few healthy treats like baby carrots, blueberries, broccoli florets, plain yogurt, and a few low-fat doggy treats, or use your pet's regular kibble for training.

The most difficult part of loving a large dog may be the short lifespan. The bigger the dog, the shorter her lifespan and the sooner she is likely to age and develop the diseases of aging, like heart disease and cancer. Giant and some large breeds are considered seniors at about six years of age. A Chihuahua may not slow down until well beyond twice that many years, and some small dogs live into their 20s. Giant breeds have a lifespan of approximately ten years, some even less.

Part 1

Small dogs have a separate set of bone and joint problems. Tiny pets like Affenpinschers and Cavalier King Charles Spaniels are more prone to luxating patellas (kneecaps slipping out of place) and slipped stifles (knee joints slipping out of place). Small dogs often suffer from arthritis as seniors and are not tolerant of extreme weather conditions. Your toy dog must live inside the house with you! Small dogs are also more fragile, especially as puppies. A jump from a high couch or the arms of a child could result in leg fractures in a Pomeranian, Italian Greyhound, Miniature Pinscher, Papillion, Toy Poodle, Chihuahua, or any other small, light-boned puppy.

Your Dog's Color

As mentioned above, dogs with large amounts of white, like Dalmatians and Beagles, are more prone to hereditary deafness. Color can influence your pet in other ways, too. Black dogs are less heat tolerant because their coat absorbs heat. Your black Lab may become dangerously overheated long before his brother, the yellow Lab. Rottweilers look tough but are notoriously intolerant of high temperatures, and small black dogs like Affenpinschers and Manchester Terriers can quickly develop heatstroke on a hot summer day out in the sun.

Light-colored dogs may not feel hot as quickly, but their light coats may offer less sun protection. Dogs get sunburned, too, and can even develop skin cancer. Don't let your white Poodle, your Bichon, your red Miniature Pinscher, or any light-colored dog sunbathe for too long without first applying a canine sunscreen spray (yes, they make it!).

Small breeds, like Chihuahuas, can easily injure their fragile bones.

Light-colored dogs may need more sun protection.

Whose Hues?

Match the color with the breed. Do you know whose hue is whose?

1. Great Pyrenees	A. Golden-red
2. Rhodesian Ridgeback	B. Any color, any pattern
3. Schipperke	C. Wheat-colored
4. Finnish Spitz	D. Black
5. Weimeraner	E. Mahogany-red
6. Irish Setter	F. Grey
7. Greyhound	G. White

. * See the end of this chapter for the right answers.

Dogs love to be part of their human's life.

How Do Dogs Think?

You can examine your dog's coat, his paws, his ears, even his teeth, but you can't examine the canine brain just by looking. While dog anatomy and even dog genetics are well understood, what goes on in the canine brain remains largely a matter of speculation. No one can really say with certainty how a dog thinks in the way they can say how a dog breathes, digests, or heals. However, animal behaviorists do know a lot about how dogs behave and how they are likely to behave.

One of the more convincing theories about the canine thought process is that dogs think in images. Not having language, as we do, but being intelligent nevertheless, dogs probably think in a way similar to humans before they used language. Dogs have visual, aural, tactile, taste, and smell images from their environments. They remember these images, both the pleasant ones, like you lavishing affection or giving treats, and the unpleasant ones, like you yelling or leaving.

But they don't speak. Sure, they can understand the meanings of certain words. Some dogs even know hundreds of words, and their humans claim they seem to understand the gist of conversations going on in the room. That may indeed be true, but not because dogs possess language. Dogs get the "gist" because they understand the images. They remember that whenever you come home, you pet and praise them. They remember that when you get a certain tone of voice or when you walk to the closet where the leashes are kept, a treat or a walk or a trip to the park are probably imminent. They also might associate an image of the car with an unpleasant trip to the vet or feel fear at the auditory "image" of thunder, yelling, a certain breed of dog, or even a small child, depending on the past imagery associated with that thing.

So what does that mean for our relationship with dogs? How do we use this information for better communication?

Do We Need to Think Like a Dog?

Dogs are creatures of habit, and they like routines. They are also smart enough to remember things they like and try to make them happen again, and they remember things they don't like and try to avoid them. Understanding how this works is critical to teaching your dog what you want her to do, as well as what you don't want her to do.

Dogs are creatures of habit who enjoy doing the same activities.

The first key is to understand why your dog does the things he does. Did he chew up your shoe when you were late coming home because he was mad at you? Behaviorist William E. Campbell suggests that instead, your dog didn't get the pleasant image of you coming home when he expected it, so he's trying to get some kind of experience of you in place of the real deal. Did he defecate on the floor to get you back for being so busy or did your apparent withholding of affection cause him so much stress that he lost control?

You must let your dog know what to expect in your household.

Sobering Statistics

According to the Humane Society of the US, 8 to 10 million dogs and cats enter animal shelters every year. Three to five million of those dogs and cats are adopted, but four to five million of those are euthanized every year, and many of the dogs and cats adopted from shelters are returned to shelters because their owners weren't properly prepared for the responsibility of pet ownership.

If you know what your dog expects and what causes him distress, then you will be less likely to yell at him for things he didn't do "on purpose." Yelling or, even worse, hitting your dog is extremely confusing and damaging to your relationship. He'll have an image of you yelling or doling out pain, but he won't be clear why. Seemingly random, frightening behavior from you will eventually erode your relationship with your dog. He'll lose trust in you, you'll think he's untrainable, and boom…one more dog abandoned to the animal shelter, where chances are slim that he'll be re-adopted.

Can't We All Just Get Along?

Thinking like a dog can indeed help you and your dog to get along, agree on some house rules and mutually beneficial behavior, and maintain a lifelong fulfilling relationship. First, don't set your dog up to fail. Don't leave things around that he will tend to destroy. Give him things with your smell on them that he is allowed to chew—but not shoes, because then he'll think shoes are OK for chewing. Pay attention to your dog and what his habits and tendencies are so you can redirect his behavior when necessary. You can't just ignore your dog and expect him to know how to behave.

You can also make imagery work for you. If you know your dog gets overly emotional when you leave, make it a habit *not* to make a big deal before leaving or when coming home, so your transition times are calm rather than dramatic. Socialize your dog by giving him lots of positive images associated with all kinds of people, animals, and situations. Save the negative imagery for direct links to behavior you don't like, such as a very quick sharp "No!" if he tries to bolt out the front door. Don't yell at him when he comes back after running out the door, or he'll think you are angry at him for coming back.

Later in this book you'll get more specific directions on training, but for now, just keep in mind that your dog probably thinks in images and in terms of positive and negative associations with those images, and you'll be on your way to better communication and a firm foundation for a strong human-canine relationship.

Think, But Don't Act, Like a Dog

The last key to your dog's mind to keep in *your* mind is that while you will benefit from knowing how your dog thinks, you won't benefit from acting like your dog. Some books tell you to behave like a member of the pack, but trainer Gary Wilkes explains that this is the worst thing a human can do, because dogs are faster and have sharper teeth. If your dog thinks you are just another dog, he may try to challenge you. However, if he thinks you are some kind of super dog, with the amazing talent to walk on two legs and make all kinds of fascinating vocal inflections, expressions, and movements, if he thinks that he could never ever be as amazing and powerful

Your dog should associate positive things with you and your family.

Your dog will respect you if you take on the role of leader.

as you, then he'll feel safe and confident that you are in control. He won't have to be.

The trick is to act like an assertive but kind *human being,* one who understands dogs—their motivations, their desires, their fears, and their needs—but is bigger and better and smarter than a dog.

You can do that.

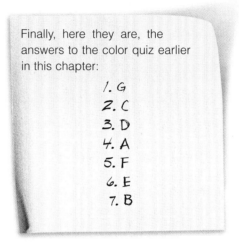

Finally, here they are, the answers to the color quiz earlier in this chapter:

1. G
2. C
3. D
4. A
5. F
6. E
7. B

Creating a Dog

It's easy to find a dog. Just visit the local animal shelter or scan breeder ads on the Internet. But what about making your own dog–taking this dog and that dog and giving nature a little nudge?

Actually, whether or not to breed your dog is hardly a joking matter. It might sound like fun to have a litter of puppies rolling around in the living room, and sure, it is fun to have puppies around…some of the time. But what about when one of those puppies is stillborn or the mother needs a Cesarean section? What happens if the mother doesn't feel like feeding or nurturing her puppies? Are you ready to be up every two hours around the clock bottle feeding ten hungry mouths? What about housetraining ten puppies, or even

Breeding your dog is a big responsibility.

Only healthy and even-tempered dogs should be bred.

two? What if you can't find homes for all those adorable puppies, and suddenly you've got seven gangly over-enthusiastic adolescent dogs barreling through the living room, their cute fuzzy roly-poly days a dim memory?

Breeding is a serious, and certainly not profitable, endeavor. It involves a massive commitment of time and emotional and financial resources. It often involves heartbreak. While people once believed dogs were healthier if bred at least once, veterinarians know this isn't true. In fact, dogs that are neutered (spayed or castrated) before ever mating enjoy a host of health benefits and are easier to manage as pets, as well.

Nevertheless, people continue to enter the dog-breeding hobby, and if they didn't, healthy, sound purebred dogs would eventually die out. We don't want that! On the other hand, we also don't want dogs bred in puppy mills without human interaction or regard to their health and welfare. We don't want females used as breeding machines for years on end. We don't want dogs languishing in pet store kennels for months because nobody happens to want that kind of puppy at that time. And we don't want purebred dogs for sale that aren't healthy with stable temperaments.

The simple truth is that nobody breeds dogs responsibly and well and makes any money at it. It's just not a cost-effective hobby. So why do people do it? Because they are totally devoted to the purebred dogs they breed, so much so that they are willing to endure the hardships associated with purebred dog breeding. Unless you are willing to commit to purebred dog breeding by learning everything you can about it (see the Resource section for some good books on the subject), including becoming an expert in dog genetics, health tests for genetic medical conditions, and puppy socialization, please reconsider breeding your pet. There are millions of dogs in animal shelters waiting for good homes. The world doesn't need any more puppies produced without careful planning. Instead, please consider having your pet neutered.

Responsible breeders require that those pups they sell as pets–the majority, since most litters produce only a few, if any, puppies that have the makings of a great show dog–must be spayed or neutered. Animal shelters require this of their adoptees, too. But if you take a puppy from a friend, find a stray, or buy one from a pet store or a breeder who doesn't require it, should you have your pet spayed or neutered? Is it worth the cost, the risk of anesthesia, the recovery time? Are you stealing away your dog's "manhood" or "womanhood"?

Yes, yes, yes, and absolutely not.

Why Neuter?

You all know the guy–or maybe you *are* the guy–who just can't get himself to have his male dog castrated because he somehow feels it is a betrayal to a brother. Or what about the family that just "didn't get around to it" and wound up with a pregnant female, sire unknown? The benefits of having your pet neutered are numerous. Once a male dog has done "the deed," he is never quite the same. Now he knows what he is missing, and he will be driven by the quest for more. His motivation to reach a female "in season" can result in some extraordinary accomplishments–think: leaping tall buildings with a single bound.

Most breeders will require that you neuter your pet-quality puppy.

Fixed Up
According to the American Pet Products Manufacturers Association (APPMA) 2001-2002 National Pet Owners Survey, seven out of ten pet dogs are spayed or neutered.

A dog that has never tasted the pleasure of canine copulation won't know what he is missing and will be much happier to hang around with you at home. Wouldn't you rather have your dog more focused on you than on every nearby female in season, as well as more focused on the job at hand, whatever that may be: your training session, the agility obstacle course ahead, hiking up a mountain at your side, or sitting on your feet watching Animal Planet?

Breeding requires the best care for both the mother and the resulting puppies.

Spayed females make better pets, too. Unspayed females go through a twice-yearly menstrual cycle, which can get messy, especially if your dog has a long and/or light-colored coat. You'll need to invest in special canine pads or diapers to keep your girl from bleeding on the furniture or the carpet. Pregnancy and whelping can be very difficult for some females, and some have no interest in caring for their puppies, which means you get to do it! An unspayed female will go into season twice a year, and if you don't keep yours secluded from the highly motivated male dogs in the neighborhood, the resultant puppies will be your responsibility. Plus, spayed females often shed only once a year instead of twice a year.

Neutering can calm both males and females and make both less likely to wander (though not less territorial about the property line). Some people believe neutering makes dogs more affectionate. Neutering does *not* make your dog fatter, however. Proper diet and plenty of exercise will keep any dog in shape, neutered or not. Plus, neutering offers health benefits for both males and females, including a decreased risk of tumors of the reproductive organs.

To Breed or Not to Breed?

So you still think your total devotion to Pomeranians or Pekingese or Pugs would make you an excellent dog breeder? Did you know all three breeds have a particularly high incidence of Cesarean births and may be prone to other serious difficulties with labor? Some dogs have very difficult, painful labors. Greyhounds have been known to "scream" during delivery. Labor may involve a lot of blood, fetal death, death of the mother, or other emergencies. So much for the "beautiful miracle of birth" you thought your children should witness! On the other hand, some births go easily. Not all canine birth is fraught with disaster. Some dogs make excellent mothers, and all their pups thrive.

But let's backtrack for a minute and look at the big picture. What does it mean to breed a litter of dogs? Considering the number of unwanted dogs in the world, what is the purpose behind breeding?

Purebred dog fanciers believe that the only reason dogs should be bred is to improve the breed. That means making a careful study of canine genetics and other health issues relevant to your breed. Both dam (mother) and sire (father) should be healthy with good temperaments, closely matching the breed standard for that breed.

Breeding responsibly also means having the parents of the litter screened for genetic disorders like hip dysplasia (common in large breeds), progressive retinal atrophy (common in many breeds), von Willebrand's disease (a bleeding disorder common in some breeds), luxating patellas (slipped kneecaps), or whatever other disorders are common for your breed, and providing documentation of these tests to those who will take home the puppies.

Most breeders also spend time and money showing their top prospects in the dog show ring in order to put championships on their dogs, showing that a puppy comes from good stock. While champions in a pedigree (the written record of a dog's genealogy, back three generations or more) are no guarantee that a dog will be healthy with good temperament, they do indicate that the dog may be more likely to come from good genetic stock and will probably be close to the breed standard. But getting championships on a dog isn't easy. The dog show world is competitive, expensive, and (dare I say it) political.

Probably the best way to help you decide if you are ready for everything dog breeding entails is to visit a few dog shows and get to know some dog breeders who are willing to talk to you or, better

High Standards

The breed standard is a written description of the ideal specimen of a particular breed. Typically, the breed standard describes the ideal dog's height and/or weight, body and head shape, ear and tail carriage, coat type and color, and many other detailed aspects of the dog's conformation, movement, and temperament. Breeders committed to improving their breed of choice carefully study the breed standard and choose a dam and a sire they believe will produce the best possible puppies. The AKC and the UKC list breed standards for many breeds on their websites. National breed clubs are also a good source for your favorite breed's written standard.

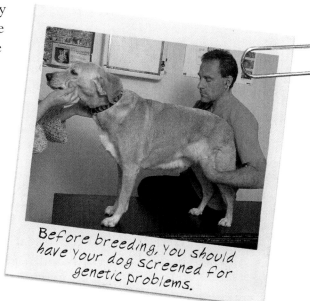

Before breeding, you should have your dog screened for genetic problems.

yet, take you on as an apprentice. Once you've seen the day-to-day life of a dog breeder firsthand, you'll have a much better sense of whether or not it's something you are willing to do. A few good mentors are invaluable to teaching you the ropes and helping you to learn everything you need to know about your breed and how to contribute to its improvement.

OFA

The Orthopedic Foundation for Animals (OFA) keeps voluntary database information on the incidence of genetic diseases in purebred dogs. Animals registered with OFA can have it on record that they are free of hip dysplasia, elbow dysplasia, autoimmune thyroiditis, congenital cardiac disease, and patella luxation. Those who breed dogs prone to any of these conditions can help to ensure the improved health of future generations of purebred dogs by having their dogs tested for these conditions and registered in OFA's database.

Last of all, if you are truly committed to responsible breeding, consider joining a local or national breed club so you can have the benefit of their resources, including the latest information on scientific developments, canine genetics, tests, and innovations, and anything else that can make you a better breeder and your puppies healthier, happier, and more perfect.

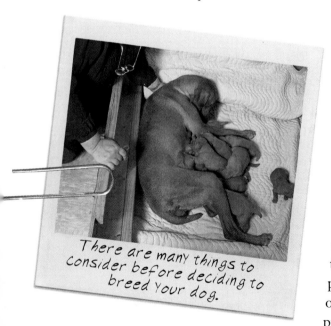

There are many things to consider before deciding to breed your dog.

The Ethics of Dog Breeding

Is dog breeding the "right" thing to do? Many people question whether dog breeding is necessary at all anymore, considering the euthanasia statistics in our country. Some believe breeders should be strictly regulated, and some call for the end of purebred dogs, period.

Purebred dog breeders who truly love their breed work diligently to improve the health and temperaments, not to mention the working ability and consequent correct conformation of the dogs our world knows and loves. Yet some people believe losing purebred dogs is worth saving those dogs who are abused by puppy mills and other for-profit breeders who pay no attention to the health and welfare of the dogs they bring into the world. Others believe that while purebred dogs per se aren't necessary, humans should be able

Part 1

to continue to breed dogs to do the jobs we need them to do, as we have always done–farm work, herding, pulling a sled, or working as service dogs, search and rescue dogs, therapy dogs, or companions.

Only you can decide if dog breeding is the right thing for you, or anyone else, to do. If you do decide to become a dog breeder, however, please do so with the commitment to gaining all the knowledge necessary to improve, not just continue, the dogs you bring into the world. Many breeders believe that the only ethical way to breed dogs is to consider yourself responsible for every puppy you cause to be produced throughout its entire life. These breeders typically have contracts that state buyers must return the dogs they purchase to the breeder at any time during their lives, no matter how old the dogs are, rather than take them to an animal shelter.

These breeders have decided to take on the responsibility for the health and welfare of every puppy they help to create, from the initial choosing of the dam and sire to the necessary genetic testing, puppy socialization, and careful choosing of buyers. If no dog was ever produced except under circumstances like this, pet overpopulation would probably be only a vague memory.

Dogs and the Law

Several websites keep track of ongoing legislation related to dogs, the banning of certain breeds, and the regulation of breeders. One of these organizations, whose purpose is to defend the rights of people to keep all breeds of dogs responsibly, is the American Dog Owner's Association, Inc. Check out their website at www.adoa.org/. Also check out Dog Watch at http://www.dogwatch.net/, a site that keeps track of breed-specific legislation.

Make sure you are knowledgeable about your dog's health before breeding.

How can this dream become reality? Regulations on dog breeding that punish mismanagement and irresponsible breeding practices but that don't punish responsible breeders who work hard for the betterment of dogs are probably a great place to start, but so far, most proposed regulations don't work well to distinguish quality breeders from those who breed for profit. Keep an eye on the news, though. Dog-related legislation is popping up all over–some of it helpful, some of it hurtful. The more you know, the better you'll be able to make informed choices.

Do You Have the Right Stuff?

Before we leave the question of whether to breed behind and move on to some guidelines for beginning breeders, please consider whether you are willing and able to endure, abide by, and live with the following conditions, questions, and situations so integral to the life of a responsible and ethical dog breeder. If you have doubts about your willingness to accept any of the items on this list, please seriously reconsider your plans to breed your dog:

√ Do you know what genetic and other health problems are common in your breed?

√ Have you taken the right steps to prevent these conditions in your puppies, including paying for the necessary tests to certify that the parents are healthy?

√ Are you committed to continued learning about the genetic health of your breed?

√ Are you familiar with the breed standard for your breed? Do you understand why the standard is written the way it is according to your breed's original purpose?

√ Do you understand how to use the breed standard to produce better puppies? Are you committed to doing so?

√ If the mating doesn't take, are you prepared for the disappointment and the expense of trying it all again?

√ Are you ready to watch your female dog go through a lot of pain and trauma so often associated with labor?

√ Are you informed about false pregnancy in dogs? Do you know what to do?

√ Are you ready to pay for emergency care during labor, including a Cesarean section, if necessary?

√ Are you prepared to deal with stillborn puppies or young puppies that fail to thrive and die?

√ Are you prepared for the expense of vaccinating all the puppies and having them checked by a vet, no matter how many there are?

√ Are you ready to be up every few hours day and night no matter how you feel or what else is on your schedule to feed the puppies during that time between weaning and getting the puppies accustomed to regular kibble?

√ How do you feel about the constant scooping of puppy poop?

√ Are you prepared to find good homes for all the puppies, and to keep those puppies you can't place?

√ Are you prepared to have and enforce spay/neuter contracts for all the puppies you place as pets?

√ Are you prepared to take back any of the puppies you helped to create if their owners can't keep them, no matter when, how old, or how sick those puppies may be?

√ Are you prepared to socialize the puppies from birth by gentle handling and interaction so they are already well prepared for life with humans when you place them?

If you breed your dog, you will be responsible for the well-being of the puppies.

√ Have you considered becoming involved with breed rescue?

√ Are you prepared to lose money at this endeavor, just because you love dogs?

√ Are you prepared to provide a loving home for every animal in your care throughout its lifetime? (Of course, any pet owner should be prepared for this one, not just breeders!)

Canine Health

The American Kennel Club Canine Health Foundation (AKCCHF) and the Morris Animal Foundation are two organizations devoted to canine health and genetics that work closely with dog breeders to fund research and provide information to research scientists. The AKCCHF and the Morris Animal Foundation have helped to uncover and disseminate much helpful information, including the discovery of many genetic markers for inherited disease and the development of tests to determine what dogs are affected. You can contribute to or even join these organizations, which have websites and newsletters. Check them out:

American Kennel Club Canine Health Foundation
251 W. Garfield Road, Suite 160
Aurora, OH 44202-8856
(888) 682-9696
e-mail: akcchf@aol.com
website: www.akcchf.org

Morris Animal Foundation
45 Inverness Drive East
Englewood, Colorado 80112-5480
(800) 243-2345
(303) 790-2345
website: www.morrisanimalfoundation.org

Guidelines for Beginning Breeders

For those of you who are still with me, still ready, still committed, and still prepared to enter into the world of dog breeding, there are many good books that go into great detail about all that is involved in breeding dogs. Such extensive information on dog breeding is beyond the scope of this book, but here are some guidelines to get beginners started.

Pregnancy and Prenatal Care

Maybe you planned a breeding, or maybe... whoops...your dog has become pregnant without you intending such a thing. Either way, you'll be best prepared to meet your canine friend's needs if you know exactly what to expect when your dog is expecting.

But are you sure she's pregnant? When a female dog is pregnant, she doesn't "show" until about the fifth of her nine weeks of gestating those puppies. At this time, she will experience a puffy abdomen, breast enlargement, and increasing discomfort as those puppies grow bigger–in fact, many of the same symptoms pregnant humans experience. Some muscular and/or deep-chested dogs may hardly show at all, and if your dog suddenly goes into labor when you didn't even know she was pregnant, you wouldn't be the first astounded pet owner.

Puppies won't start moving around until the final week of gestation, but your dog may experience an increase in appetite and increasing crankiness, although many other conditions can cause such behavioral changes.

If you are an experienced breeder awaiting a special planned litter, you may want to invest in a pregnancy test or an ultrasound. Talk to your vet about these options. Accidental breeders probably won't want to spend the money on these luxuries–save up for the possibility of a problematic labor instead!

If your female is indeed pregnant, she'll need lots of good nutrition during her pregnancy, just as a human would, especially during the final four weeks of pregnancy, when she should be eating approximately 20 to 40 percent more than normal. Just like a human, canines can also get morning sickness and may not feel like eating. Your dog may vomit, and this is normal unless it goes on for more than a week or more than a couple of times a day. Ask your vet about the canine equivalent of prenatal vitamins and what foods to try if your expectant mama doesn't feel much like eating, but don't go overboard on any one nutrient. Too much of a vitamin like vitamin A or a mineral like calcium can cause health problems for both puppies and mother.

Pregnant females should continue to get regular exercise, but nothing dangerous or overly strenuous, especially as her abdomen begins to expand. A too-active pregnant female could become injured trying tough athletic feats because her weight and balance is changing.

She probably won't mind a little extra pampering, either, to get her through the discomfort, although many females become so uncomfortable that they want to be touched and

A pregnant dog needs regular checkups to ensure all is well.

Is She or Isn't She?

Some female dogs experience a condition called *pseudocyesis* or *false pregnancy*, a condition in which the dog experiences hormone-induced symptoms of pregnancy without actually being pregnant. Mild cases usually resolve on their own. You'll know your dog isn't pregnant when signs of pregnancy simply subside. Chronic false pregnancy can be treated with medication and after a cycle is resolved, spaying. Also, having an actual litter of puppies sometimes puts an end to chronic false pregnancies.

Puppies-to-Be for Sale!

During those 63 days of waiting, you have plenty to do securing good homes for the puppies. Don't wait until the litter is born to start your search or you may not find homes in time. Experienced breeders planning litters often take deposits on puppies even before the actual breeding. Even if your dog became pregnant by accident, work on finding the puppies good homes before they are born.

You should provide a special space and a whelping box for your dog.

doted on only on their own terms. Respect your pregnant dog's space and mood.

Your Canine Birthing Room

You should also plan for the whelping, or birth of the puppies, by providing a space and an appropriate whelping box.

Labor can be long and tiring. Mothering is even more tiring, and those tiny puppies need to stay warm, dry, and secure. Before your dog goes into labor, figure out where the whelping should happen and build or buy a whelping box.

Choose an area that is relatively secluded and warm, not in the center of the action of the household. The size of the whelping box depends on the size of your dog and the puppies. Whelping boxes for larger dogs could be about five feet by four feet. Toy dogs can get by with a whelping box of approximately two feet by three feet. Some dogs prefer a more enclosed space like a crate.

Ideally, a whelping box should have a side that lowers for the mother to go in and out easily, but that raises up again and latches in place to keep the puppies inside. A ledge around the inside to keep the mother from accidentally pressing puppies against the walls is nice, and so is a hinged roof over part of the box for extra shelter. Don't set a frame over a bare floor. Instead, build or set the whelping box on a pallet or plywood base and cover it with comfortable bedding. Clamp a heat lamp on the side and place a baby scale nearby, and you've got your birthing room ready to go.

Let your dog get used to the whelping box by encouraging her to spend pleasant time in there eating, sleeping, and playing, at least two weeks before whelping so that once the time comes, she feels secure in her space.

Part 1

And then one day, just about nine weeks after conception, labor begins. Those puppies are coming, ready or not…and you'd better be ready!

Whelping

It's time! It's time! It's time! While you may feel the prospect of delivering a litter of puppies yourself is daunting at best, unless you encounter an emergency, you should be able to handle the birth at home. If it is timed right, you can certainly take your dog to the vet or emergency veterinary clinic to handle it, but if you plan to be a real breeder, you'd better learn how to do it yourself.

Every breeder should have certain whelping supplies on hand. Before labor begins, make sure your birthing room is stocked with:

√ Lots of clean hand towels

√ A stack of newspapers

√ Trash bags

√ Clamps or hemostats

√ Latex gloves

√ Dental floss for tying off the umbilical cord if necessary

√ A clock

√ Petroleum jelly to help lubricate the birth canal if a puppy gets stuck

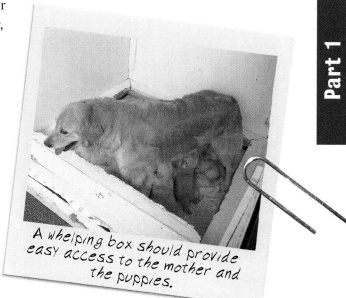

A whelping box should provide easy access to the mother and the puppies.

Build Your Own

Many breeders build their own whelping boxes. One Australian Shepherd breeder has an Internet site with plans for a whelping box you can print out to build your own. Check it out at:
http://www.geocities.com/Heartland/Valley/1198/whlpbox.html.

√ A thermometer

√ Alcohol for disinfectant

√ A styptic pencil

√ A book on dog breeding that you've already read at least once, for reference

√ Paper and pen for writing down birth times and weights

√ Bottles and newborn puppy formula, just in case mom won't nurse

√ Plenty of accessible water for the laboring mother

How do you know when labor has begun? Pregnant females give several indications that labor is imminent, although every dog is different. Some may pant, nest by vigorously shredding and tearing apart the bedding in the whelping box, alternate between deep sleep and restlessness, become especially clingy, or even shriek dramatically.

Each puppy has its own placenta, which many females eat or try to eat. The mother should also tear and lick the puppy's umbilical cord, but if she is too vigorous, she could cause hemorrhaging. If the puppy is bleeding excessively or the mother has bitten the umbilical cord too closely, clamp off the umbilical cord and apply the styptic pencil to stop the bleeding. Puppies should want to nurse immediately. If the mother isn't doing her duty, be ready to feed those newborn mouths.

Some mothers wait and rest for up to two or three hours between puppies. Others shoot them out one after the other. At the end, when the final placenta is delivered, a final puppy may surprise you, too. When labor is all over, the mother should curl protectively around the puppies to sleep soundly and nurse. Most mothers do a good job, but

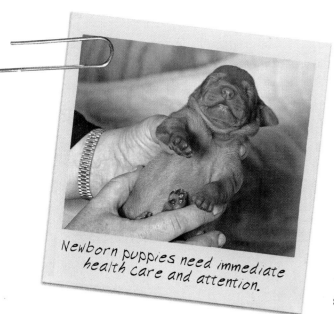

Newborn puppies need immediate health care and attention.

String of Puppies

Puppies are in a dog's uterus in a long string of sacks like sausages. As each puppy comes out, the mother (or you, if the mother doesn't seem inclined) must immediately clear the sack away from the puppy's airways and rub it vigorously to initiate breathing.

The mother will take care of most of the puppies' needs.

a few have no apparent maternal instinct. Pugs are known for this, although some Pugs make fine mamas. When your dog refuses to be the mom, you get to do all the post-natal caretaking.

As the labor progresses, keep careful records. Write down each puppy's birth weight (you have your infant scale nearby, right?), make notes on any distinguishing characteristics, and see if you can tell if the puppy is a male or a female. The male should have a tiny penis just under the umbilical cord, and a female should have a tiny vulva between the back legs. If labor is moving quickly or if the puppies are very small, it may be hard to tell the sex of the puppies until a little later.

When labor is over, offer the mother a light but nutritious treat like beef broth and make sure she still has plenty of water if she needs it. Then, let her sleep. Make sure she is caring for all the puppies and keeping them warm. She'll even lick up their feces for the first week or two.

Meanwhile, you can celebrate (or take a much-needed nap yourself)!

Aftercare for Mother

After labor, your work is far from done. The mother must see a vet within 24 hours after labor. She'll need a shot of oxytocin so everything is properly expelled and can start to shrink back down to normal size. She'll also need to be checked to make sure she doesn't have any infection or other postpartum problem. She probably won't want to leave the litter, and when you take her to the vet, be sure someone stays with the litter. New puppies must stay warm and fed or they can quickly perish.

In the first few weeks after giving birth, dogs can experience several serious health problems, so watch your new mother carefully for signs of illness, such as fever, shivering, listlessness, failure to take care of the puppies, swollen breast tissue, red or pus-filled discharge from breasts or vagina, aggression, or other behavioral changes. Some common postpartum disorders include:

Mastitis, a breast infection caused by engorgement or a blocked milk duct. The breast will become hard, red, hot, painful, and possibly caked with crusted milk and/or pus. Milk can become discolored or full of pus and puppies shouldn't nurse from an infected breast. Take your dog to the vet, who will prescribe antibiotics and possibly pain medication. Warm compresses can help ease the pain. Prevent mastitis by making sure each breast is emptied twice a day, either by puppies or by your hand.

Healthy parents will ensure healthy puppies.

Eclampsia, sometimes called *milk fever,* an emergency condition that usually develops in the first few weeks after labor. Caused by a calcium deficiency due to inadequate parathyroid hormone, the hormone responsible for mobilizing calcium in the system, eclampsia's symptoms include nervousness, salivation, quick breathing, whining, staggering, muscle twitching, and shivering, as well as abnormal behavior, including aggression toward puppies. Eclampsia can be fatal and must be treated by a vet. If eclampsia occurs, puppies must usually be hand-fed.

Acute endometritis, a serious infection of the uterine lining accompanied by fever, vaginal discharge, and an unpleasant odor.

Lack of appetite, suppressed milk production, and depression are signs of this condition, which can be caused by failure to pass a fetus or placenta or by a labor-related infection. If you suspect your dog has a uterine infection, take her to the vet immediately.

In most cases, luckily, your dog will be just fine as long as she takes it easy and as long as you give her lots of care, love, and attention. If your new mother wants to be left alone, leave her alone. If she wants you to leave the puppies alone (more common in the first few days), leave them alone when she is in the whelping box. If she doesn't want to hang around with the puppies and would rather be with you, indulge her. Spend lots of time by the whelping box while she nurses, but give her some one-on-one time, too. She deserves it!

Newborn Care

In many cases, the mother will take good care of her puppies all the way to weaning, but that doesn't mean you don't have to keep an eye out for what's going on in that warm little whelping box. Sometimes things can go wrong, and you must be ready. And, before you know it, boisterous little pups will be clamoring over the sides and into the big wide world.

If there is a problem with the mother, you may have to hand feed the puppies.

The first four weeks after birth are the most crucial for your tiny puppies. Keep the heat lamp warming the whelping box but make sure you adjust it so it doesn't overheat or burn anyone. Puppies must never be allowed to get cold in their early days. Let a vet check your new puppies to be sure each one is free of health defects or is treated for those that can be treated.

Sometimes, puppies don't make it, either for serious, obvious reasons such as fatal birth defects, or for less obvious reasons, such as the umbrella term "fading puppy syndrome." If you provide the mother and her pups with everything they need, nature will do the rest. Some puppies simply won't make it no matter what you do. In many cases, however, most or all of the puppies will be fine.

A Tale of the Tail

Many breeds, such as Rottweilers, Dobermans, Schipperkes, Vizslas, and Miniature Pinschers, traditionally have their tails docked. Your vet can perform this minor surgery within the first two to three days after birth. After that, the procedure isn't recommended, as it becomes major surgery. Many vets now refuse to dock tails as well as to crop ears on healthy non-working dogs, and many states outlaw even newborn tail docking by breeders because it is considered the practice of veterinary medicine. Many traditionally docked and cropped dogs are showing up undocked and uncropped as pet owners and fanciers become less willing to surgically alter their pets for cosmetic reasons. Several countries such as Germany and Sweden have outlawed docking and cropping, but these procedures remain legal for vets to perform in the US and Canada. The issue is highly controversial and many vets, breeders, and pet owners have strong opinions on the subject.

Keep a watchful eye on where the puppies are–keep counting–so a tired, stressed, distracted, or suddenly panicky mother doesn't accidentally smother or kill a puppy. You also have a few other chores that mama dog can't take care of herself:

Every day:

√ Check and count all the puppies.

√ Make sure everyone is actively feeding. If a puppy seems limp or weak, manually put him onto the mother's breast or, if that doesn't work, begin hand feeding.

√ Make sure everyone is behaving normally. Pups who won't nurse, whose bodies are limp, or who seem frantic or hyperactive and cry constantly may be failing to thrive. Let a vet check them out.

√ Make sure everyone is warm. If a puppy gets chilled, warm it first, then feed it. A puppy is in danger of death if its temperature falls below 94 degrees. Puppies pant if overheated.

√ Clean any crusted feces or food off puppies.

√ Wipe down whelping box.

√ Weigh everyone.

√ Gently handle every puppy every day. Puppies who receive positive human interaction from birth are well socialized to humans.

Every week:

√ Snip off the sharp ends of every puppy nail with a small clipper made for dogs, including dewclaws.

At three weeks:

√ Around three to four weeks, many mothers begin to wean their puppies, some quickly, some very gradually. Provide a pan of gruel for puppies. Over the next five to six weeks, thicken the gruel, eventually adding ground up puppy food of gradually increasing chunk size until your puppies are eating regular puppy food.

Now that your pups are growing big and strong and developing sparkling personalities of their own, don't forget to handle and play with the puppies every day, introducing them to lots of interesting and different people, animals, and situations to help them become the happiest, most well-adjusted puppies they can be. Soon you'll hand over the responsibilities of your puppy's health and welfare to someone else, but think how lucky you've been to have those joyful little fellows in your life. And how lucky they've been to have you!

Newborn pups should see a vet to begin vaccinations.

Pups in Dreamland

Newborn puppies sleep 90 percent of the day and nurse 10 percent of the day. Puppy eyes open between one and two weeks of age, making sleep pretty easy during those early days.

Part Two

A Healthy Foundation

"I'm sorry, Ben, but you can't have any more pig's feet until you finish your kibble."

Training and Socialization for a Longer Life

Although this isn't a training book, you may wonder what dog training has to do with health. Nothing you do for your dog will have a greater impact on his health and welfare than being well trained and well socialized. Behavioral problems are a major reason why pet dogs are relinquished to animal shelters, and a dog in a shelter is probably not headed down the road of good health and a long life. Sadly, many puppies never see their first birthday because they weren't trained and got into more trouble than their owners were willing to handle. If you don't teach your puppy what kind of behavior is acceptable to humans, he won't be successful living with humans. It's as simple as that.

Every dog can benefit from basic obedience.

Patience and consistency are the keys to training.

We humans aren't very tolerant of bad or even normal canine behavior. Our untrained canine friends may bark to alert us of every suspicious piece of trash that blows down the street. They may use the house as a bathroom, because that's what we do, right? They may chew on our shoes when we aren't home because it reminds them of us. And what do we do? We get angry, they get confused, the behavior worsens, and many of us, sad to say, give up. A badly behaved puppy won't grow up to be a well-behaved and successful human companion…and may not grow up at all.

If your dog doesn't know the house rules and can't behave in a way that you can live with, the relationship won't work. That's why it is absolutely essential to train your dog, preferably in a professional setting.

How to Train a Dog

Dog training may sound easy, but many who come home with a dog for the first time don't have the first idea how to start. If you've seen those dogs on television trotting neatly around the show ring, leaping over hurdles in an agility race, or sitting, lying down, and shaking hands on command, you may wonder how on earth anyone was ever able to communicate the information about what they wanted to a creature that doesn't speak your language.

In essence, communication is exactly what dog training is all about. Because dogs don't speak and we aren't practiced in the nuances of canine communication, training gives dogs and humans a mutual sort of "language" through which to communicate.

There are many different methods of training. Clicker training, lure and reward training, and traditional or "military" training are a few of the most popular. If you aren't a professional trainer, however, you may find it difficult to grasp the concepts behind these different methods, which are concepts rooted in study of canine behavior. That's why it's best to begin at the beginning–that's where your puppy is beginning, too.

Training Techniques

Clicker training is a type of training that uses a little, hand-held plastic box with a metal tab that makes a clicking sound when pressed. The trainer uses the click to precisely mark a behavior, and the behavior is then rewarded. Clicker training separates the reward from the behavior with the precise sound of the click, making it perfectly clear to your dog which behaviors you like. For more information on clicker training, see clicker trainer Gary Wilkes' comprehensive website at www.clickandtreat.com. **Lure and reward** training uses a treat to lure a dog into certain behaviors like sits, downs, come, and even through obstacle course equipment. **Traditional** or **military training** is the older style of dog training in which dogs are taught commands through repetition and are corrected for mistakes, usually with a so-called "choke" chain. Each method has its benefits and different dogs/human teams respond best to different methods.

Treats and praise can motivate your dog.

Puppy Kindergarten

Puppy kindergarten classes are a great way to begin socializing and training your new puppy. These informal classes don't focus on hard-core training. Instead, they act more as an aid to socialization. A group of people brings in their puppies, and everyone gets to interact, learn about basic dog care and training, and expose the puppies to lots of different people and, of course, other dogs.

Puppy kindergarten classes are available in most cities and towns. They are positive and fun in character and everyone has a great time, sometimes forging lifelong friendships with others whose dogs get along. Consider it a structured and educational playgroup for puppies.

Basic Obedience

Once your puppy has graduated from puppy kindergarten, it's time to move on to basic obedience. If you never take another class, don't skip this one. This is the class where you

Puppy classes are a great place to socialize your dog.

and your dog will learn how to communicate what you would like him to do. Because most dogs are highly motivated to please their owners, not to mention doing whatever it takes to get a tasty treat, some simple techniques make it easy for you to show your dog what you mean by "sit," "stay," "come," and other essentials.

In basic obedience, you and your dog construct the bare bones of training communication that will allow you to either move on to more advanced training, if you enjoy it, or simply communicate more successfully at home. Basic obedience instructors typically teach you how to train your dog to sit, lie down, stay, come, and walk next to you without pulling on the leash. You will also get helpful hints about advanced training and typical behavior problems. You'll learn a lot, and if you find a good instructor, basic obedience classes are worth every penny.

A good obedience instructor is someone who uses positive methods but is flexible enough to adapt or switch methods if one method isn't working for you and your dog. If your trainer is adamant that all dogs respond best to traditional training or clicker training, for example, you may find that you and your dog won't be successful in class.

Watch a couple of classes if possible before you sign up, and get recommendations, too. When watching classes or talking to friends who have taken classes, look for a few key signs that you've found a good obedience instructor:

√ Do you get the impression that both people and dogs are having a good time? If the class isn't fun, neither you nor your dog will keep up with the necessary practice.

√ Is the instructor friendly with good people skills? Even if he loves dogs more than anything else in the world and is able to train dogs himself to the highest levels of competitive obedience, an instructor who can't communicate well with people or who doesn't enjoy people probably won't do a good job at training you. People training is just as important in basic obedience as dog training.

√ Does the instructor obviously enjoy her job? An irritable or impatient instructor is unpleasant to work with.

√ Do you like the way the instructor interacts with the dogs? If you feel like the instructor is too rough on the dogs, and/or if you aren't comfortable with the methods you see, look elsewhere. You probably haven't found the class for you.

Basic obedience is essential for every dog because it gives humans and their dogs a set of rules and signs through which they can come to an understanding. This is how everybody learns how to live together. If you decide to continue on to more advanced canine competitions, like competitive obedience, agility (a competition where dogs run an obstacle course), flyball (a fast-paced canine relay race), or even the show ring, you and your dog must first master the basics. After all, you can't play a piano concerto unless you first learn your scales!

But even if you aren't interested in moving on to competition with your friend, basic

There are many types of competition that you and your dog can enter.

Canine Competition

Basic obedience classes frequently offer introductions to competitive obedience, agility, conformation shows, and other fun canine competitions. The obedience instructor may explain how these competitions work, or even let you and your dogs try out agility equipment. Basic obedience is necessary for any advanced canine competition, so get the basics down first, then consider the possibilities for future fun together by enlisting in a local obedience or agility club and buddying up to those experienced in the canine sport of your choice.

obedience is the key to a society in which dogs are well behaved and well managed by their owners. This is the key to decreasing the number of dog attacks and dog nuisance problems that give so many dogs and dog owners a bad name. More dogs would be allowed in parks, on beaches, in hotels, and in apartments if they were better behaved, and

Basic obedience allows your dog to participate in activities with you.

Who's Training Whom?

A dog trainer is the person training a dog, so if you and your dog take an obedience class together, you will be the dog trainer. The person teaching you *and* your dog how to communicate is the obedience instructor. If you hire someone to train your dog for you, that person is also called a trainer. This can be handy, and particular effective for problem dogs, but in most cases, your relationship with your dog will benefit most if you are the trainer, not someone else who won't live with your dog. After all, isn't that why you got a dog, for the relationship? Work through the training together and you'll both be closer, more knowledgeable, and better behaved when interacting with each other.

basic obedience is the first step toward demonstrating to the world that your dog is a good citizen.

Canine Good Citizen® Award

When competitive obedience first became an event, the purpose was for dogs and their people to demonstrate what good manners they had. In fact, the basic obedience title is called a CD, which stands for Companion Dog, meaning that a dog that has earned this title has all the qualities of a good companion.

As obedience progressed and became more competitive, another program emerged that allows "regular" (in other words, not necessarily purebred) pets, no matter their breed or age, to demonstrate that they, too, can be good canine citizens. The American Kennel Club's Canine Good Citizen® Program awards a nice certificate and the CGC® "title" to dogs who pass a ten-item test administered all over the country by trained evaluators. You and your dog can master the ten basic tests in a basic obedience class or in widely available Canine Good Citizen® training classes. Want to get a head start on a CGC® for your dog? The following are the ten tests. If your dog fails any one of these tests, he will be dismissed but can try the test again on a different day as many different times as necessary.

Test Item 1: Accepting a friendly stranger.
Your dog must stay in position next to you and behave, i.e., not act shy or resentful, when the evaluator approaches and shakes your hand in a friendly manner.

Test Item 2: Sitting politely for petting.
Your dog must stand in place and allow the evaluator to pet her in a friendly way without acting shy or resentful.

Test Item 3: Appearance and grooming.
Your dog must be in good health and stand politely for brushing, combing, and a physical examination of his ears and feet by the evaluator.

Test Item 4: Out for a walk on a loose lead.
Your dog must walk beside you on either side on a leash and remain attentive and responsive to you as you walk her around the testing area, following the evaluator's directions for a right turn, a left turn, an about turn, a stop and start, with or without sitting during the stops.

Test Item 5: Walking through a crowd.
Your dog must walk on a leash next to you through an area containing pedestrian traffic without getting overly excited, shy, or resentful, and without jumping on anyone or straining on the leash.

Test Item 6: Sit and down on command–staying in place.
Your dog must show that he can sit and lie down on command. Then, with your dog on a 20-foot leash, you must tell your dog to stay and walk forward to the length of the leash, turn, and return back to your dog. Your dog must stay in place when you do this until you release him at the evaluator's cue.

Test Item 7: Coming when called.
Your dog must stay while you walk away for ten feet, then turn to face her. When you call your dog, she must come to you.

Test Item 8: Reaction to another dog.
Your dog must be polite and show no more than casual interest in another dog as another handler and dog come up to you in a friendly manner and stop, shake hands, and chat. Neither dog should move to go to the other dog or to the handlers during this test.

Can You Hold It, Please?

If your dog eliminates during any of the Canine Good Citizen® tests except the last one (and only then if the test is outside), she will be disqualified and you'll have to try again on another day. Make sure your dog has a chance to go *before* you begin the test!

Part 2

Test Item 9: Reaction to distraction.

Your dog must remain confident and interested or curious or even slightly startled by distractions, such as a jogger, another canine, or a rolling dolly. Your dog must not react in a panicked, aggressive, or overly startled manner and should not bark at the distraction.

Test Item 10: Supervised separation.

Your dog must tolerate supervision by a trusted person. The evaluator will approach you in a friendly manner and ask you if you would like him or her to watch your dog. You agree, then the evaluator takes the leash. You must then go out of sight of your dog for three minutes. Your dog needn't maintain a position but should not bark, whine, or pace unnecessarily or act otherwise nervous or traumatized. Mild agitation and nervousness is permitted.

That's the test. Easy? Sure it is, with the right obedience training and lots of practice. All tests are performed on a leash and may be inside or outside. And remember, you can always try the test again…and again…and again, until your buddy has earned the unofficial but nevertheless prestigious title of CGC®.

Teach your dog the household rules from the beginning.

Housetraining and Other Rules

One of the most important things pet owners learn during puppy kindergarten and basic obedience is how to teach a dog some basic house rules. No puppy (or human for that matter) is born knowing what is and isn't appropriate in the house, so it's your job as a canine guardian to make those rules clear.

As mentioned at the beginning of this chapter, failure to learn house rules is one of the main reasons that dogs end up in animal shelters, but in most cases, if your dog doesn't know the rules, the owner is at fault. Once again, classes are incredibly important because the obedience instructor trains both you and your dog about how to interact and communicate. If you have proven effective strategies to help housetrain, control excessive barking and chewing, and fix other non-human-friendly doggy behaviors, you'll be set up to succeed.

While classes are usually the best environment for any dog-human team to learn together, here are some helpful hints and strategies for controlling some common canine behaviors you probably don't like very much. Just remember, every dog-human team is different. What works for one dog may not work for another, so be flexible, patient, and positive in your approach. Eventually you'll find a method that works for both of you.

Oops, He Did It Again!

The one thing puppies do that most irritates humans has to be those unfortunate accidents of elimination…you know, those little "surprises" your puppy leaves for you when you aren't paying attention, and those little puddles all over the kitchen floor in the morning.

Puppies have no idea where it is appropriate to eliminate, but think about it: neither do human babies. We put diapers on them for a couple of years, but your smart little pup will figure out where it's OK to go and where it's not OK to go in a matter of just a few months. Some quick studies learn within a few weeks of bringing them home (this also depends on the age of your puppy when you bring him home, how much housetraining the breeder or previous owners have already accomplished, and what breed you have).

Patience is certainly in order when it comes to housetraining your puppy, but don't expect your pup to figure out the rules all by himself. Some handy tools and helpful rules will get

Teacher's Pet

Many good books and videos give you directions for training your dog, but in my opinion, there is no substitute for a hands-on class or private sessions with a great dog trainer who can watch you and your dog and give you personalized suggestions and corrections. Look for a trainer who uses positive rather than punitive measures and is flexible enough to adapt training styles to meet the needs of you and your dog. Let books, dog magazines, and videos serve as supplementary information because, of course, the more you know, the better a dog trainer you'll be.

Housetraining allows your dog to live with your family.

Crate training is the fastest and easiest way to housetrain your dog.

Your dog will soon consider his crate

your puppy in shape in no time, and the most powerful housetraining tool you can have is a crate.

A crate is great! Choose a plastic or wire crate just big enough for puppy to sit, stand, turn around, and lie down in, but not so big that he can soil in one side and sleep in another. Nylabone® makes a Fold-Away Pet Carrier that convientently folds up for easy storage.

Crate training is one of the most reliable housetraining methods, and it's simple. Dogs love to have a den-like area where they can go for downtime whenever they need it. Because dogs don't soil where they sleep, keep your puppy in his crate whenever you cannot directly supervise him.

Of course, that doesn't mean leaving him in there all day long. No puppy can hold it for more than a few hours, and you'll just be setting him up to fail. Puppies should come into a home where someone is often around and can watch and direct most of the time, but when it's nap time or you need to get something done, put him in his comfy crate and shut the door. He may cry at first, but he'll soon learn to see his crate as a place of refuge *as long as you never use the crate for punishment.* Let it be a haven.

When your puppy is out of his crate, watch him carefully for sniffing and circling behavior, then take him quickly outside to the spot you'd like to train him to use for his personal potty. When he goes, associate the action with a word (pick one you won't regret later–"potty" is OK, but some other words I can think of could prove awkward should the neighbors overhear).

Tiny Tyrants

Toy dogs are notoriously more difficult to housetrain than larger dogs, possibly because their owners tend to let them lord it over the house and they may figure that if humans get to go inside, why shouldn't they? I remember an Italian Greyhound that would only use the human bathroom as his potty and stubbornly refused to go anywhere else. My grandmother's toy Poodle, Bitsy, has her own bathroom in the house and uses the shower for her personal toilet. It makes for easy cleanup, and my grandma, who can't get around much, doesn't have to walk her. Some people also love the new dog litterboxes for small dogs. They use a special paper-based pelleted litter, and you can train your toy dog to use them just as you would train to use a spot outside. Work with your dog and your lifestyle, and you will soon convince your tiny tyrant to adopt bathroom habits you can live with.

Part 2

When he does his duty, praise him effusively. Always take your puppy out about a half hour after eating (sooner if he starts to circle and sniff), and as soon as you take him out of his crate. Wait outside with him until he goes so you can mark the behavior with the word and then deliver the praise. A few weeks of this and he should get the idea. If you are consistent and never let your puppy fail by having an accident because you are always watching, he'll learn quickly.

If you fail your pup by missing his signals, and he has an accident in the house, *it's your fault*. Please don't blame your puppy. He won't understand why you are angry, and you could seriously damage your relationship. Remember to communicate with him through methods he understands. If he knows where you want him to eliminate, that's what he'll do, unless he absolutely can't hold it any longer, you don't get the signal to let him out, or if he simply doesn't yet understand what you want.

Your puppy will show signs that he has to eliminate, like sniffing and circling.

Chewing and play biting should be controlled while your dog is young.

Play Biting and Chewing

Everyone with a puppy knows about those needle-sharp teeth. Puppy bites hurt! The problem is that your puppy doesn't know that. Puppies play together, biting and chewing on their littermates, and because dog skin is less sensitive than human skin, the other pups don't seem to mind much. We humans, on the other hand, don't like puppy bites, but pet owners often tend to overlook the irritation of those sharp little teeth because the puppy is just so darned cute.

Bad idea.

Dogs must learn at an early age that biting human skin is a big NO. That means reacting with a sharp sound and pulling back every single time the puppy's teeth hit human skin. Your puppy won't like this startling reaction, and it teaches your puppy bite inhibition. An adult dog with bite inhibition that is well socialized to lots of different kinds of people will be far less likely to bite.

Dog Bites Man

According to the American Veterinary Medical Association*:

• As many as 1 million people annually require medical treatment for dog bites. Dog attacks send more than 334,000 people to the emergency room each year.

• One million people report dog attacks each year; millions more go unreported.

• About 12 people each year die from dog attacks.

• Dog attacks cost society $1 billion annually.

• According to the Insurance Information Institute, insurance companies paid $250 million for dog bite liability claims in 1996 alone.

• State Farm Fire and Casualty Company paid nearly $80 million in dog bite-related claims in 1997.

• Reported dog attacks have increased at a rate of two percent annually, according to the Insurance Information Institute, and 37 percent from 1986 to 1994 (National Center for Injury Prevention).

*These facts are courtesy of the American Veterinary Medical Association's website and can be reviewed on the Internet at http://www.avma.org/press/dogbite/factsheet.asp.

These statistics send a clear message to dog owners: keep your dog healthy, on a leash, well socialized, well supervised, and teach bite inhibition early!

Puppy Party

Socializing your dog is one of the best ways to keep her well adjusted. After your pup has had her first few rounds of vaccinations, host a puppy party. Invite lots of different people of various ages and appearances to come to your house and meet your dog. Let people pet her and talk to her one at a time while you supervise so that every human interaction is positive. But don't stop there. Take your puppy with you whenever you go out (when possible) so she is also exposed to different places and different situations. The more positive and varied experiences she has in the first year, the more well adjusted, flexible, and stable she will be.

As for chewing, some breeds and some individual dogs are more apt to chew destructively than others, but in general, you can prevent your dog from chewing destructively by doing a few simple things:

√ Give your dog plenty of toys he is allowed to chew. Make sure some are challenging, like Nylabone® Rhino® toys and other stuffable toys filled with treats, peanut butter, or other temptations that are mentally as well as orally stimulating.

Nylabones® are a safe chewing alternative for your dog.

Part 2

Toys and bones can be given as a reward for a job well done.

√ Keep your dog busy! Bored dogs are more likely to engage in destructive chewing. Up your dog's daily exercise and give him more attention.

√ When you can't supervise your dog, let him rest in his crate or in a safe place where he can't destroy anything.

√ Don't leave your dog alone for more than a few hours, though. Come home from work on your lunch hour to take him on a walk or hire a dog walker to do it for you. Remember, wear him out, and he'll be too tired to chew your shoes.

√ Keep your shoes and other things you don't want your dog to chew out of his reach. Prevention of the behavior always works best.

Jumping Up

Dogs love to be with us, and when we get home after a long day, they want to see us…up close! Puppies often learn that jumping up on their owners is just fine. We are flattered that our cute, fuzzy little fellows love us so much that they practically try to climb up to get to us.

However, when that fuzzy little fellow grows to be a 75-pound bruiser, jumping up isn't so cute. It can even be dangerous, especially to a small child or an elderly or petite adult. Just as puppies must learn bite inhibition early, they must also learn that jumping won't get them anything good, but that sitting politely will.

The problem with this lesson is that it's hard for humans to teach. When we get home after a busy day, a dog jumping on us is likely to get our attention, even if that attention is negative and involves lots of yelling. That's

Most dogs jump up to greet people.

Old Dogs, New Tricks

If you adopt an older dog that has a jumping problem, you can institute this same technique. Ignore him by turning your back to him and calmly and quietly say, "No." If you have to push the dog off you and make him sit, fine, but don't make a big, loud deal about it. Just do it quietly and in a neutral way. Once he's sitting nicely, then shower him with kudos. Old dogs *can* learn new tricks with a little patience.

Allow your dog to sit nicely for attention and praise him for his good manners.

still attention to your dog and preferable to being ignored. A nice polite dog that sits patiently is easy to ignore or forget about, so we inadvertently tend to reinforce the jumping up with attention, while failing to reinforce the behavior we so prize.

Starting in puppyhood, when your puppy jumps on you it is crucial to either completely ignore her or tell her "No" firmly and tell her to "Sit." When she sits, lavish her with praise and give her the attention she craves. If jumping up is never rewarded in any way, including with yelling, your dog will soon stop doing it. If sitting nicely for petting when greeting people is always rewarded, that's exactly what your dog will learn to do. Dogs are smart. They know what they want. Make it easy for them to understand how they can get your attention, and they'll behave just the way you would like them to.

Barking…and Barking…and Barking

Most dogs bark. All dogs make some kind of noise, even the so-called "barkless" Basenji. Dogs have been bred over the centuries to bark for different reasons. Herding dogs

Problem behaviors like barking can be caused by boredom.

Part 2

Bark Stress

Excessive barking can actually damage your dog's health by injuring his vocal chords. Perhaps even more insidiously, excessive barking, especially when it becomes obsessive and chronic, could contribute to excessive anxiety, a heightened physical state that stresses your dog's system in ways that could have a number of negative effects, possibly even compromising the effectiveness of your dog's immune system to fight disease. Of course, if your dog is barking out of boredom or separation anxiety or due to a health problem, first resolve the problem, which could be causing your dog much more stress than the actual barking symptom.

bark to keep the flocks in line. Terriers bark to indicate where that pesky vermin is hiding. Hounds bark to indicate that they have found what they are looking for. Guardian dogs (most dogs, for that matter) bark to warn of intruders.

Barking is integral to what a dog is, and that means that to some extent, if you plan to live with a dog, you have to put up with some barking. On the other hand, there is a limit.

Just like people, some dogs are pretty intuitive about when barking is really necessary and when it's not. They may bark if a stranger approaches the property, but will completely ignore the blue jay in the tree because they know it isn't a threat and they aren't going to be able to get to it, anyway. Other dogs tend to be a bit more...shall we say chatty? They bark at everything–any people, anywhere; any other dogs; local wildlife; dog toys; wind; air. Some breeds are more prone to excessive barking. Terriers tend to be particularly "barky," making them less well suited for apartment living, especially when the walls are thin and the neighbors aren't amused by the sound of constant barking–can you say "eviction notice?"

Then there are dogs that get in the habit of barking, and it becomes almost like a compulsive behavior. Other dogs are simply bored. They don't have anything else to do and they enjoy barking, so they do it. Still other dogs are nervous, either because they are unsocialized or are left alone too often, and become fanatical about the approach of anything to their property, barking frantically at any movement. These last few types of barkers have problems you can address.

Because you can indeed be evicted or otherwise charged when your dog becomes a legitimate nuisance to your neighbors, and because compulsive or excessive barking is actually stressful on your dog and can result in ill health, you must, as a responsible dog owner, help your dog stop excessive barking. You can do this in several ways:

√ Stop rewarding your dog for barking. If she barks and you yell, she may interpret your yelling as reinforcement, almost as if you are barking in agreement. Instead, quietly and calmly remove her from the source and put her in her kennel or in a room alone. When she is quiet, praise her.

√ Minimize distractions. Don't let your dog sit and look out the window if it makes her bark too much. If you see another dog approaching on a walk or someone walking by your yard and your dog starts to get excited, immediately call her to come to you and have her sit. Pet her calmly and praise her. Hold her collar and reassure her that you saw the approaching intruder and she has done her job. If she struggles and barks, don't get excited and "bark back" again. Remain uninteresting and non-interactive until she is quiet again.

√ Don't leave your dog outside and ignore her for long periods of time if she tends to stand outside and bark or patrol the property line obsessively. Let her be inside with you. She'd rather be there, anyway.

√ Keep your dog busy. Give her more interesting things to do when you are away, such as lots of toys stuffed with treats to play with.

√ Leave the radio or television on when you leave if it keeps your dog distracted. Background noise can also drown out noises from outside that may trigger barking.

√ Keep your dog in her crate when you are away so she can't get to the window. Her "den" will keep her calmer and she won't feel responsible for having to scare away all those "intruders" she sees passing on the street.

Ignore your dog when he barks and reward him when he is quiet.

√ Make sure your dog gets lots of exercise before you leave for the day. A long morning walk is a good solution.

√ If you live in a residential area, don't leave your dog outside when you are gone if he tends to bark. You can't supervise your dog outside if you are gone, anyway, and he could be stolen, teased, or otherwise goaded into trouble by passersby.

√ Try a humane bark collar, such as one that sprays citronella when a dog barks. Dogs don't like the smell of the spray (it doesn't spray them in the face, but they can still smell it), so it deters them from barking. Other options for less sensitive dogs include electronic vibration collars or static shock collars that correct a dog for barking. Talk to your vet about options and always read and follow instructions on the collar to avoid improper use.

As a Last Resort

In extreme cases, you can have your dog surgically "de-barked," but I would never recommend this unless your dog is at risk of being euthanized due to barking or you are at risk of suffering legal action and nothing else has worked. Try everything else first. This procedure alters your dog's vocal chords in a way that drastically lowers the volume of his barking but doesn't eliminate it.

Digging and Other Destruction

Some dogs love to dig, particularly terriers (terrier means "earth dog"), but hounds, working breeds, and herding breeds are notorious diggers, too. Any breed and any dog may enjoy digging. It's fun, it's interesting, it's satisfying. What's not to love?

At least that's your dog's point of view. If you have flowerbeds or even just a nice lawn, you aren't going to want your dog to dig it up. Holes from digging are hazardous to human ankles and don't exactly contribute to a lovely landscape.

Some dogs are dedicated diggers, but you can usually at least reduce, if not eliminate, digging behavior with a few key strategies:

√ Keep your dog well exercised and busy. Many dogs dig because they have excess energy or because they are bored.

√ Give your dogs challenging things to do. If they are mentally stimulated with toys from which they must work to extract treats or from complex training sessions with you, they will be less likely to feel the need to dig.

√ Keep your dog inside when you aren't supervising him in the yard.

√ Fence off areas tempting to your dog, such as flowerbeds and vegetable gardens.

√ Use dog repellent to keep your dog away from certain areas you can't fence off. Your pet store should supply dog repellent, usually in spray form. Read and follow the instructions on the package.

√ If you are building a fence, pour concrete along the base to keep your dog from digging under, or at least bury the fence 6-12 inches underground (depending on how persistent a digger your dog is).

Fear and Anxiety

If your dog is fearful, either around new situations, people, and noises or if she's always afraid of the same thing (fireworks, the vacuum cleaner, you leaving her), that fear is harmful to her health because it causes her so much stress. It is also damaging to your relationship. Fear makes dogs do things we don't like, such as suffer housetraining accidents, destroy things, claw madly at doors, whine and cry, or cling to us, pathetically shivering. Some dogs can also become fear biters who will attack out of panic. That means someone could get seriously injured, you could get in big legal trouble, and your dog, sad to say, might pay the ultimate price.

Many different methods exist for conquering fear and anxiety in dogs. Some behaviorists recommend desensitization, in which the animal is exposed to noises, strangers, or whatever the source of fear is just a little at a time. This method works on the same

Some dogs are born to dig, especially terriers.

Part 2

When You Just Gotta Dig

Sometimes, it's easier to go with the flow and give your dog a chance to dig. Designate an area, perhaps a plastic swimming pool filled with sand or a square of dirt marked off by railroad ties, for your dog to dig. If she learns that digging in her special area is OK, she'll be able to exercise her need to dig without upsetting you. Everybody wins!

Toys can help curb your dog's separation blues.

principle as socialization for puppies. The more your dog is exposed to something, the more familiar and the less scary it becomes. In extreme cases of fear or anxiety, consult a trainer or canine behaviorist specializing in anxiety. Your vet may also want to prescribe medication to help calm your dog.

However, in the case of separation anxiety, a condition in which your dog becomes fearful and often destructive when you leave, it is best handled a bit differently. Experts suggest ignoring your dog for the ten minutes before you leave and the ten minutes before you come home. Although you may find this difficult to do, this process sends your dog the message that your coming and going aren't exciting or stressful or overly emotional in any way. Big shows of affection, petting, and fawning over your dog ("Is Zuzu going to MISS Mommy when she goes away? Because Zuzu LOVES Mommy? Yes she does! Yes she does!) will only make these transitions more emotional and stressful for your dog.

When you do come home, after you have ignored your dog for about ten minutes, then you can give her a pat on the head, a few kind words. Work up to the smushy kissy affection after you've been home for awhile, so your buddy doesn't associate it with your leaving or coming home. Again, for severe separation anxiety, see your vet. Your dog could have an underlying medical problem or might require medication to help relax him so you can better treat the problem.

On the Run

Do you call your dog Harry Houdini because he can escape from everywhere? Whether she leaps over fences in a single bound or can dig out like the Poky

Keep your dog in a fenced-in area at all times.

Little Puppy, some dogs have an unquenchable wanderlust. Of course, a loose dog is in great danger. Your wayward pup could be hit by a car, stolen, or attacked by another dog or even a wild animal. The best way to keep your pet from escaping is simply to thwart him. As a responsible pet owner, you must keep your pet from running free, even if it means extending the height of your fence, pouring concrete around the base of your fence, or taking your dog on long walks instead of letting him roam around the backyard unsupervised.

And if you don't have a fence? Please keep your dog safe and don't let him out without a leash.

Basic Training Tips

While learning basic training under the personal guidance of an experienced obedience instructor is usually best, you can set the groundwork for basic obedience moves on your own using these tips. Some of these methods may not work for every dog, but young puppies will usually respond well.

SIT: Take a piece of kibble or a tiny bit of hot dog or cheese and hold it in front of your puppy's nose so he gets a good whiff. Then slowly move the treat up and over his head. He'll have to sit to see it. When he does, say, "Sit," then praise him and give him the treat. Repeat and he'll soon associate the movement with the word. For a long sit, keep him sitting for slightly longer periods of time before giving him the treat. Always let him succeed—give him the treat *just before* he is ready to give up and stand up again.

DOWN: Lure your puppy into a sit, then pull the treat out and down. As he follows the treat with his nose, he'll have to creep forward. Help guide him into a lying-down position with your other hand while keeping the treat about an inch in front of his nose. For a long down, keep him in the position for slightly longer periods of time before giving him the treat. Again, always let him succeed by giving him the treat before he gives up and stands again.

STAY: After your puppy has mastered sit and down, lure him into one of these positions, then hold your palm up and say, "Stay." Take one step away. If he jumps up, put him back into position and again say, "Stay" with your palm up. Only make him stay a couple of seconds the first time. Then step forward, praise him, and give him the treat. Extend the stay time for a couple of seconds and step back another step every few times. Go back to your puppy to give him the treat rather than having him come to you at first, so he doesn't confuse the "Stay" with "Come." With this method, your buddy will be specifically rewarded for staying and not for coming to you.

COME: Teach your puppy the come command by practicing many times each day. Call her to you and reward her with a toy, a treat, or lots of affection when she comes. Eventually you can combine "Stay" and "Come" by making your puppy stay, stepping back, then releasing her with a "Come" or "Here," or whatever word you choose, and let her come to get the treat.

Exercise is one way to solve many behavior problems.

Trained, socialized, well behaved? Your dog has a great start to a long healthy life. Keep up that training and keep building that relationship and you'll both enjoy your time together even more.

How to Feed Your Dog

Dogs eat dog food. That sounds simple enough, but actually the type of food, how much is fed, and the manner in which it is fed to your dog can all have a drastic impact on your pet's health and longevity. As your dog's guardian, it is your job to make sure he gets the right amount of protein, vitamins, minerals, fats, and calories to stay fit and healthy. Obesity is a common problem among pet dogs, but even dogs at a healthy weight may not be getting optimum nutrition, because the foods they eat don't provide them with enough absorbable protein for their needs, enough fat for their coats, or the right carbohydrates to facilitate energy and digestion.

A balanced diet is the key ingredient to good health.

Choose a diet that best fits your dog's age and activity level.

Dogs Love Treats

Everybody loves treats, and your dog is no exception, but a treat doesn't have to come from a pet store. You can find healthy additions to your dog's diet right in your own refrigerator...in the produce bin! Avoid fattening treats to keep your dog in optimal health. Instead, see how many of the following non-fat, high-fiber, nutrient-packed goodies your dog enjoys (limit to two per day for small dogs to ensure they don't fill up and shun their regular balanced diet):

√ Raw baby carrots

√ Broccoli florets

√ Green beans, cooked or raw

√ Peas

√ Seedless grapes

√ Blueberries

This chapter will help you to determine exactly what your dog needs and what your dog's food should contain. If you've never peeked at that dog food label before, it's time to drag out that bag of kibble or that can of meaty chunks and take a good hard look. Keep that label with you as you read this chapter. You'll want to refer to it often.

Your Dog's Dietary Needs

Dogs are not humans (obviously). Humans are omnivorous, meaning we need a balance of meat and plant foods to stay healthy, and arguably, our diets should contain primarily plant foods with just a little meat for digestible protein.

Dogs, on the other hand, are carnivorous. Unlike our flat human teeth, dog's teeth are long and sharp, custom-made for eating meat. Dogs have a shorter intestinal tract, stronger stomach acid, and a different mix of enzymes made for digesting meat.

That doesn't mean your dog shouldn't eat any plant food. Dogs need fiber, carbohydrates, and fats from plant foods, as well as the vitamins and minerals plants contain. But, the primary source of protein in a dog's diet should be meat, and the first (ideally, the first two or even three) ingredients on your dog's food bag should come from meat. A food that lists cornmeal, rice, or some other grain as the first ingredient may not have the available protein a meat-based food will have, but corn or rice or oats as a third or fourth ingredient is fine, providing your dog with fiber, vitamins, minerals, and fatty acids from vegetable oil.

Digestibility

Further complicating the picture is the fact that not all proteins are created equally. Some proteins are more digestible than others. Proteins from muscle meat are highly digestible. Grains contain less protein than animal products, and their protein is also less digestible. Likewise, proteins from animal by-products may or may not be as digestible as muscle meat.

Just because a dog food contains a certain percentage of protein doesn't mean your dog will actually use that much protein, and while some dog foods boast digestibility statistics (82- to 86-percent digestibility is about as high as is possible for high-quality protein, although some manufacturers have been known to exaggerate that number on their packaging), that information is not required by law. Neither are the contents of a "by-product" or "by-product meal" or even "meat meal." In other words, the dog food label is informative, but it may not tell you everything you really want to know.

Treats should be nutritious and part of your dog's regular diet.

A healthy diet includes the essential proteins, vitamins, and minerals.

Part 2

How do you know how digestible your dog's food is? Look for a food that lists regular meat or meat meal as the first ingredient, and meat, meat meal, meat by-products, or meat by-product meal as the second and even the third ingredient. If the third or fourth ingredient is a grain, you've probably got a food with high digestibility. Higher-priced "premium" or "super-premium" foods are more likely to contain higher quality, digestible proteins than "economy" foods. Look at the label nevertheless. A few of the more expensive brands do list grains as the first ingredients and may also include a lot of preservatives and sugar. Best to stick with those that list meat first and at least one other meat source second or third.

> ### AAFCO Says
>
> Every dog food intended for use as a primary diet should contain a statement that it has been tested and approved for use as a food in all life stages. The group that sets guidelines for pet foods is called the American Association of Feed Control Officials, known as AAFCO by those in the biz. AAFCO sets minimum protein, vitamin, and mineral limits for pet foods. While no law requires pet foods to follow AAFCO's standards, it has become an industry policy and most companies do so. They can then state on their label that they meet AAFCO standards.

A well-balanced diet is the foundation of good health.

Beyond Protein

Dogs need more than protein. They need fat and carbohydrates for energy. While dogs (and people) can use protein for energy in a pinch, fats and carbs are more efficient energy sources, and allow for the body to use protein to build and repair itself.

Dogs can manufacturer most fatty acids on their own except for linoleic acid (omega-6) that they must ingest. Linoleic acid is important for keeping your dog healthy, because it keeps your dog's skin, nose, paw pads, and coat soft, pliable, and shiny. Meats and grain oils contain linoleic acid.

Carbohydrates supply glucose to cells, which not only supply the body with energy but also help digestion and keep muscles and the brain in good working order. Simple carbohydrates make for quick energy. These come from grains like corn, rice, and oatmeal. Complex carbohydrates like cellulose are a good source of fiber, which regulates water in your dog's large intestine and keeps your dog's bowels moving efficiently. Dog foods may contain other sources of fiber, too.

Dogs require 14 vitamins: Thiamin (B1), Riboflavin (B2), Pantothenic acid (B5), Pyridoxine (B6), Niacin, Vitamin B12, Folic acid, Biotin, Choline, Vitamin C, Vitamin A, Vitamin D, Vitamin E, and Vitamin K. They also require the minerals calcium, phosphorus, magnesium, sulfur, iron, copper, zinc, manganese, iodine, selenium, and cobalt.

The vitamin and mineral balance your dog requires is tough to figure out on your own, so relying on a complete fortified dog food may be the best way to keep your dog's diet nutritionally sound. If you make your own dog food, you'll need to make sure these vitamins and minerals are present in the proper proportions. If you feed a quality dog food, that balance should already be in place.

All About Dog Food

Let's look at that dog food label again. You'll see lots of different things listed there, and you probably don't know what they all are. Manufacturers are required to list ingredients by dry-weight amount, meaning the most prevalent ingredient is listed first. However, if a grain is broken down into parts, such as ground corn and corn gluten meal or wheat flour, wheat germ meal, and wheat bran, then it can look like a food is mostly meat-based when actually the grains are the primary ingredient. Another way to make a dog food look like it contains more meat than it really

Your Dog's Daily Multi-Vitamin?

Because high-quality dog foods are typically subject to feeding trials (it should say so on the bag), they have been carefully formulated to contain just the right balance of vitamins and minerals. If you also give your dog vitamin and/or mineral supplements, you can throw off this balance, which could cause health problems for your dog. Unless you are feeding a homemade diet or your dog has a special nutritional need so that your vet recommends supplementation, leave the vitamin and mineral supplementation to the experts.

Part 2

The food you choose should be complete and appropriate for your dog.

What's In the Food?

Ingredient	What it is
Meat	Clean muscle meat from cattle, swine, sheep (or lambs), or goats, including muscle, tongue, heart, esophagus, and diaphragm.
Poultry	Clean muscle meat (as above) from chicken or turkey.
By-products	Non-rendered protein from animal carcasses not approved for human consumption, not including meat but including organs, blood, bones, fat, and intestines, and in the case of poultry, heads, feet, and undeveloped eggs. It may not contain hair, feathers, horns, beaks, teeth, or hoofs.
Meat or poultry meal	Rendered (fat removed) meal made from animal parts, containing no more than 14-percent indigestible materials. Meat meal cannot contain hair, feathers, horns, beaks, teeth, hooves, blood, skin, feces, or intestinal contents. Meat meal comes from cattle, swine, sheep, lamb, or goats. Poultry meal comes from chicken or turkeys. Meat and bone meal may also contain rendered bone.
Animal by-product meal	Rendered animal tissue that doesn't qualify as meat or (including poultry poultry meal, but which may not include any of the things excluded by-product meal):from meat or poultry meal.

does is to include many different grains in a dog food, like ground corn, rice flour, wheat flour, and soy flour. These might all be listed as the third, fourth, sixth, and seventh ingredients, but could result in a grain-based food disguised as a meat-based food.

A basic and sensible rule-of-thumb when surveying an ingredients list is to choose a food with more quality ingredients you recognize in the least processed forms: meat over meat meal; meat meal over by-product meal; ground grains over grain meal; vegetables over vegetable parts; etc.

Also avoid foods with artificial colorings and flavorings and added sugar and/or corn syrup.

Now let's look at the different forms dog food can take:

Dry Kibble

A dry kibble helps to clean your dog's teeth, and high-quality dry kibbles contain digestible proteins and all the vitamins, minerals, fats, and carbohydrates your dog requires. A good dry kibble can be an excellent source of nutrition. Kibble is cheaper than canned food (even the premium brands), and your dog doesn't have to eat as much kibble as canned food to get the same nutrition. Kibble won't spoil in your pet's food bowl if it sits there all day.

Some dry kibble is very economical, but less nutritious. Dogs on economy kibble may suffer from poor coats, skin problems, large stool volume (not fun to pick up), and other health problems especially in sensitive or allergic dogs.

Kibbles labeled "premium" or "super-premium" usually contain higher quality ingredients, but not necessarily in ideal proportions. "Natural" foods may contain more natural preservatives or other extra ingredients like herbs, digestive aids, or organic ingredients. Read the label. No law governs the use of these terms, so it's buyer beware.

Despite the high-quality nature of many dry dog foods, some people don't like the highly processed nature of kibble. The ingredients in dry kibble are often rendered into meal (processed to remove all fats and oils), then the dog food mix is processed further by going through an extruder, which mixes, heats, and then cuts and dries the kibble. Extrusion processes dog food at such a high heat that some of the proteins and vitamins are broken down and lost. Natural enzymes in the food are

How to Make a Meal

Rendering is a process in which animal meat or parts or grains are slowly heated until their fats or oils have been completely extracted, resulting in a meal: meat meal, by-product meal, or grain meal.

Dry food can help control tartar on your dog's teeth.

This Food is Clean

One benefit of the extrusion process used to create dry kibble is that the high heat completely destroys the bacteria typically found in chicken and beef. Raw home-made diets can contain bacteria like salmonella and E. coli, but kibble is sterile. Nevertheless, dry dog food is not approved for human consumption unless it says so on the label, so keep it away from your curious toddler.

Maintaining a healthy lifestyle begins with a good diet.

also destroyed. Vitamins must then be sprayed back on the food along with fat and flavoring to make the kibble taste good.

Dogs also tend to prefer the taste of canned food to a dry kibble, although other dogs are happy to wolf down anything you put in front of them (and everything you put in front of yourself, as well as everything you accidentally drop, leave on the counter, or throw in the trash). If your dog happily eats and seems to thrive on a quality dry kibble, that is a fine diet. But if your dog isn't doing well or doesn't like a dry food, consider a high-quality canned food. Just be sure to give your dog a few crunchy biscuits to keep those teeth clean.

Some people feel best about making their dog's food from scratch. If that sounds like you, then check out the section later in this chapter on making your own dog food.

Semi-Moist Food

Semi-moist foods aren't extruded so they contain more water. They also contain a lot more preservatives, colorings, and sugar to make them safe and palatable and to prevent spoilage. These added ingredients make them poor choices for good nutrition, even if your dog likes his little bone-shaped, chewy bits better than dry kibble.

Canned Food

Canned dog food contains high amounts of water. It is more expensive than dry food, and because it isn't hard, it doesn't help to clean your dog's teeth. In fact, it may even lead to tooth decay because it is more likely to stick to teeth. If you feed your dog canned food, be sure to brush her teeth regularly.

Canned food, once opened, doesn't last long and will spoil if your dog doesn't eat it right away. Your dog may have to eat more canned food to get the same nutrition, which can get pretty pricey, especially for large dogs.

Because canned food isn't extruded, it may contain more intact proteins, vitamins, and enzymes than dry kibble, and your dog is much more likely to take to canned food than to dry food. If you choose a canned food, make sure it is approved by AAFCO as a complete diet and contains quality ingredients, including fresh meat as the first two ingredients, and give your dog a healthy crunchy treat each day to help scrape plaque off her teeth.

Also, because canned food contains more water, percentages of protein, fat, and carbohydrates can't be compared with dry foods. On a dry-weight basis, canned foods actually contain more protein than dry kibble, even though it doesn't look that way on the label. Instead, compare canned foods with other canned foods to find the best nutrient profile.

Custom Formulas

Some dog foods are custom-made for dogs with certain problems or certain traits. Some lines make foods specifically formulated for small, medium, large, and giant dogs because differently sized dogs have different nutritional needs. For example, very large dogs need lower protein and calcium so that they don't grow too quickly, compromising their bone density. Fast growth in giant breeds (like Great Danes) can lead to orthopedic problems later in life. Very small dogs, on the other hand, require more frequent meals with plenty of energy, especially if they are active.

You can purchase formula if you need to hand feed your puppy.

Some dog foods are made for different types of dogs. Performance dog foods have higher protein, fat, and calories for the hardworking hunting dog, working dog (such as police or search and rescue dog), and dog athletes (such as those participating in agility, flyball, or weight pulling competitions). Senior formulas are for older dogs at risk for certain diseases of aging, or who may now be less active.

Still others are formulated for dogs with specific health problems, such as arthritis, heart disease, allergies, or obesity. Ask your vet if a custom dog food formula might be best for your dog, and don't forget to read the label. Just because it's custom-made doesn't necessarily mean it's better.

How Much, How Often?

People often wonder if they are feeding their overweight dogs too much, even though they are following the instructions on the kibble bag. While dog food does include guidelines showing you how much to feed dogs of different weights, these are guidelines only. If your dog is overweight, he is probably eating too much and exercising too little.

Most dogs simply eat too much, but every dog is different. My dog eats a lot and is skinny, probably because she is extremely active and even when she is lying still, looks like she is burning calories by worrying about things. Other dogs hardly ever exercise and remain slim, and some active dogs sport a prodigious girth.

The best way to tell if you are feeding the right amount is to look at your dog. Does he have a nice tuck below his ribs indicating a waistline? If so, he is probably in good shape. If he has no visible waistline and appears sausage-shaped, he is probably overweight. If that waist tuck is so

Your Bad Habits

People with a tendency to overeat may also have a tendency to overfeed their dogs, and overweight owners often have overweight dogs. This isn't a book about feeding yourself, but please feed your dog in a manner best suited for her health. That means feeding an adequate amount of high-quality dog food and not too many treats, including "people food" that isn't good for you either.

Table foods and snacks can lead to health problems such as obesity.

Keep Moving

Don't forget that exercise is as important a factor in preventing or reversing obesity in pets as an appropriate nutritionally sound food intake. Get that dog of yours moving every day, if not on a walk, at least for a run or romp around the yard.

extreme as to appear emaciated, he may not be getting enough food.

Another test is to feel your dog's ribs. Because dogs have different coats, you can't always tell by looking. You should be able to slightly make out the lines of the ribs in smooth-coated dogs like Greyhounds and Dobermans. In shaggier dogs, you'll have to feel your dog's ribs. Can you feel them? If so, great! If they are imperceptible, your dog may be overweight.

How Much?

Wouldn't it be nice if you could plug your dog's weight into a formula and get the exact amount of food for the perfect diet? Unfortunately, it's not that simple. The amount of food your dog needs depends on several things. First of all, the type and quality of food determines how much your dog needs. Premium and super-premium foods are more nutrient-dense than economy foods so your dog doesn't need as much. Your dog's stools should also be denser and easier to clean up on a high-quality food because more of the food is being absorbed and less extraneous material is passing through. This makes a higher quality food a pretty good deal, economically, even with the higher price tag. Canned food also differs in amount, so consult the directions, which typically provide a range depending on your dog's weight.

Always start by feeding your dog on the low end of the dog food's suggested guidelines. For example, a dry kibble might recommend 3/4 to 1 1/4 cup per day for a 15-pound dog. Start with that 3/4 cup, especially if your dog gets treats or occasional healthy people food as a supplement (or if he hangs around under your kids at the

Feed your dog at the same time every day.

Bloat Alert

Large deep-chested breeds could be at risk for bloat, a life-threatening and extremely painful disease caused by eating too quickly and gulping in air. When a dog suffers from bloat, his stomach fills with air and twists in on itself, requiring immediate surgery. Bloat seems to occur more often when dogs eat or drink quickly after vigorous exercise or tend to gulp their food. Feeding smaller amounts more often and delaying feeding until your dog is rested can help prevent bloat.

dining room table). Unless he is highly active, the low-end requirement is probably plenty. If your dog is always hungry and looks too thin, up the amount a bit. (If he is always hungry and overweight, don't give in to those pleading eyes, but do see your vet if you suspect a health problem.)

If you are unsure about whether your dog is overweight or underweight, ask your vet to help you determine your dog's status and a healthy diet and exercise plan.

How Often?

While many people feed their dogs only once a day, I know I like to eat more often than that and suspect most dogs would prefer it, too. Small dogs and especially puppies must eat more than once a day because they have small stomachs and quick metabolisms. Those little bits of food are digested quickly and waiting another 24 hours for a meal can be hard on your tiny pup.

Consult your vet if the following guidelines don't work for you because, of course, every dog is different, but for most dogs, a feeding schedule I believe works well might go something like this:

- 8 weeks to 12 weeks: 4 times per day

- 12 weeks to 6 months: 3 times per day

- 6 months to adulthood for
dogs under 15 pounds: 3 times per day

- 6 months to adulthood for
dogs over 15 pounds: 2 times per day

Part 2

Homemade Diets

Some people just feel better about making their own dog food. If you don't mind the extra work, homemade diets can be fun, but you also have to be vigilant. Even though dog food is a relatively recent invention (Ralston Purina widely marketed the first commercially prepared dog food in 1926) and 19th century pets got by on leftover table scraps, there are no studies to show how many of those dogs suffered from nutritional deficiencies. Also, remember that our 19th-century ancestors tended to eat a much healthier, less processed diet of fresh meat, grains, and vegetables. Today's leftovers aren't as healthy for our pets, just as they tend to be less healthy for us if we choose lots of processed, prepackaged, high-fat, high-sugar fare.

Commercial dog food began as a great convenience, and today it has become the norm. But if you want to cook for your precious little puppy, why not? The trick is to provide your dog with all the protein, fat, carbohydrates, vitamins, and minerals he requires in just the right proportions. Yes, dog food companies do that work for us. But plenty of people like to do it on their own.

There are excellent books go into great detail about all that is involved and all the options you have when it comes to cooking for your own dog.

Raw vs. Cooked

Many proponents of homemade diets strongly recommend using raw meat rather than cooked in the homemade dog food recipes. Raw meat contains more enzymes and, although it also contains bacteria, some believe the dog's strong digestive acids easily conquer bacteria and, in the process, the dog's immune system grows stronger. The raw meat diet also has its detractors. Not only do some people dislike handling raw meat, but the bacteria factor makes them nervous. They don't like feeding their dogs anything they couldn't eat themselves. Both methods (raw and cooked meat) have their advantages and disadvantages:

Water is an essential part of your dog's diet.

Raw V. Cooked

	Advantages	Disadvantages
Raw Meat	• more natural enzymes	• more bacteria, could harm dogs
	• quicker to prepare	• could contain harmful parasites
	• dogs like the taste	• bacteria/parasites could transfer to humans
	• more like diet in the wild	• can be unpleasant to prepare
Cooked Meat	• more pleasant to prepare	• fewer natural enzymes
	• cooking kills bacteria	• cooking could destroy other vitamins

Talk to your vet about which method might work best, but also do your own research. Only you can decide what will work best for your dog.

The Complete Nutritional Picture

Dogs cannot live on meat alone. While dogs are carnivorous, they also require many other dietary components, and if you feed your dog a homemade diet, you are responsible for making sure she gets everything she needs. This takes some research and a long-term commitment.

An initial blood test, and then a repeat test every few months when first feeding a homemade diet, can assure you (and your vet) that you are feeding your dog in a nutritionally sound manner. Are you willing to have these tests done? Are you willing to learn what you must know to give your dog everything she needs? Are you willing to mix up oatmeal, raw meat, vegetable oil, grated vegetables, bone meal, various vitamin and mineral supplements, nutritional yeast, kelp powder, and bone meal several times each week, or even every day, depending on the size and number of dogs?

If this is too much of a commitment (as it is for most of us), you are better off feeding your dog a high-quality commercially prepared food. But if you think that kind of work sounds well worth it, even fun, then go for it! You just might be amazed at how healthy and vibrant your erstwhile listless pet becomes.

When Food = Poison

You may have heard dogs have strong stomachs and can digest just about everything, but some foods are very dangerous for dogs, and some dogs are more sensitive to these foods than others. For her own health, please don't let your dog eat any of the foods on this list:

√ Chocolate—especially dark chocolate, baking chocolate, and cocoa—contains a substance called theobromine that can be toxic to dogs. Even chocolate milk can be toxic in large amounts. Always keep chocolate away from your dog!

√ Raw onions contain a chemical that can damage your dog's red blood cells and cause anemia or kidney failure.

√ Alcohol can make your dog very sick and could even put him in a coma.

√ Macadamia nuts can cause pain, stiffness, and weakness in your dog's rear legs.

√ Foods that are toxic to people: Large amounts of salt, unripe tomatoes and potatoes, spoiled or moldy food, and garbage.

Part 2

A Few Good Recipes

You may want to try your hand at some healthy additions to kibble or some homemade dog treats before committing to a completely homemade diet.

You've probably heard that people food is bad, bad, bad for dogs. That's not always true. Healthy people food can make a sensible addition to your dog's kibble, making it not only more palatable but more nutritious, adding live enzymes, fiber, healthy digestive bacteria, vitamins, and minerals to a good kibble. Just don't overdo it. Remember to keep your dog active, and even then, limit kibble additions to a maximum of one per day from the first list of high-fat additions and one to two of the low-fat additions. If your dog is very sedentary, stick to one to two low-fat additions each day.

An active dog will need a food that will meet his physical needs.

Feed the Itch

Some dogs have allergies to certain foods, most often beef, milk, wheat, soy, and chemical additives. These allergies may show up as gastrointestinal distress or in itchy, red, irritated skin. If you suspect your dog has an allergy, see your vet and ask about experimenting with your dog's diet. Switching to a different food without the offending ingredient may be all it takes to get your pet back on track to good health.

Some suggestions for kibble additions:

• 1 teaspoon to 1 tablespoon canola or olive oil

• 1 raw or scrambled egg

• 1 tablespoon ground or minced meat

• 1 tablespoon tuna (preferably sodium-reduced)

• 1 tablespoon cottage cheese (preferably sodium-reduced)

• 1 tablespoon plain yogurt

• 1 teaspoon grated cheese

• Low-fat/nonfat kibble additions:

• 1 tablespoon low-fat cottage cheese (preferably sodium-reduced)

• 1 tablespoon nonfat plain yogurt

• 1 grated carrot

• 1 tablespoon chopped broccoli

• 1 egg white

Of course, dogs love treats, so home bakers rejoice! Try these easy and delicious treat recipes. This recipe comes in the adoption package of the Iowa City/Coralville Animal Care & Adoption Center in Iowa City, Iowa, and is reprinted here with their permission.

Homemade Peanut Butter Dog Biscuits

1 $\frac{1}{2}$ cup water
$\frac{1}{2}$ cup canola oil

2 medium eggs
$\frac{1}{4}$ cup natural crunchy peanut butter
2 tbsp vanilla extract
2 $\frac{1}{2}$ cup whole wheat flour
$\frac{3}{4}$ cup unbleached white flour
1 cup cornmeal
$\frac{3}{4}$ cup rolled oats
Preheat oven to 400 degrees.

In a medium mixing bowl, combine water, canola oil, eggs, peanut butter, and vanilla extract, and stir until well blended.

In a large mixing bowl, combine wheat flour, white flour, cornmeal, and rolled oats. Add wet ingredients and mix by hand or with a mixer until smooth.

Roll dough into a ball and place on floured wax paper or a floured marble pastry board. Roll or pat to $\frac{1}{4}$ to $\frac{1}{2}$ inch thickness. Cut with a cookie cutter and place biscuits on an ungreased cookie sheet.

Bake for 20 minutes, then turn off oven and leave biscuits in oven for an additional 1 hour. Remove from oven, cool, and store in an airtight container.

Part 2

Grooming

Grooming can bring out the best in your dog: the glorious white curls of a Poodle; the gleaming ebony sheen of a Doberman; the magnificent red mane of a Pekingese; the tawny, flowing silk of a Yorkshire Terrier; the feathery ruff of a foxy Pomeranian–I could go on and on! Good grooming certainly helps your dog look beautiful, but grooming is more than just cosmetic. Grooming is an essential component to good health.

Whether your dog has a short, hard coat like a Beagle, a medium coat like a Golden Retriever, a long, showy coat like a Shih Tzu, or a coat full of curls like a Poodle or a Puli, that coat needs grooming. The skin beneath the coat needs care and attention too, as do your dog's nails, paw pads, ears,

A well-groomed appearance begins with good health.

Different coats need different levels of care.

eyes, and teeth. Grooming means more than brushing out a dog once a week and sending him on his merry way. Grooming is all about sound personal canine hygiene, and because your dog can't bathe himself, trim his own nails, brush his teeth, or treat his own skin allergies, the job falls to you.

Grooming Session How-To's

Some dogs barely need a brush and always look immaculate, while others get matted when 24 hours passes without comb to coat. But even dogs that don't necessarily need weekly grooming can benefit from it for other reasons. In most cases (except for heavily coated breeds prone to matting who need more frequent brushing), a once-a-week grooming session is a great habit for any dog-human team to cultivate.

Weekly grooming sessions give you and your dog a great opportunity to bond, and they give you the chance to check your dog over. If you give your dog an "exam" at the start of each session, you will be more likely to catch any health problems evident on her skin or coat before they get too serious. A grooming exam also accustoms your dog to the kind of handling she will get from a vet, making visits easier for everyone.

Weekly Grooming Routine

You can adapt the following steps for you and your dog. For instance, brushing is listed as the final step here, but if your dog is in serious need of coat care, and the coat is impeding access to nails, ears, and eyes, do the coat first. Because I have a smooth-coated dog, I typically save the coat for last because that's the fun part.

In general, a weekly grooming session should include the following:

First, call your dog to come to a certain spot you always use for grooming: the back porch, the bathroom, the family room, or wherever is comfortable, where you can easily reach your dog, and which can be easily cleaned afterward. For small dogs, a counter or table

Grooming Must-Haves

Every dog owner should have the following grooming supplies handy. Keeping them in a basket or tackle box in the spot where you will groom your dog makes everything easy to find:

√ Guillotine-style nail trimmers (don't use human nail trimmers on dogs)

√ Styptic pencil or other antiseptic coagulant to stop bleeding if you accidentally trim the nail's quick

√ Toothbrush tooth scrubber made for dogs

√ Toothpaste made for dogs

√ Brushes and combs appropriate for your dog's coat

√ Shampoo appropriate for your dog's coat or all-purpose, high-quality dog shampoo

√ Conditioner appropriate for your dog's coat

√ Small haircutting or nail scissors (depending on the size of your dog) for trimming excess hair from around toes and paw pads, ears, and eyes, and for clipping extra-long whiskers and neatening stray hairs around the coat

√ Blow dryer for dogs with longer coats

Part 2

with a non-slip surface is helpful. Even a card table topped with a rubber mat will do the trick, or if you want to go all the way, invest in a grooming table, which stands at just the right height.

Start by giving your dog a rubdown all over his skin, like a massage. Rub head to toe, which will help loosen dead hairs in the coat. Your dog will enjoy it, too, and if he has any lumps, bumps, dry skin patches, or sore areas, you'll find them. (If you do encounter any problems, call your vet to have them checked out.)

Next, pick up each of your dog's feet. Press on his paw pads and wiggle his toes. Doing this from puppyhood will make toenail clipping much easier when your dog is big and strong. Don't clip toenails just yet, though, so your dog doesn't associate every foot handling with toenail clipping.

Examine your dog's ears. Lift them up if they hang over. Look inside. Rub them and check for lumps. If they are dirty, clean them out with a cotton swab or cotton ball and mineral oil or special ear cleaner made for dogs. Don't stick anything way down inside a dog's ear,

Trimming your dog's nails is an important part of his grooming routine.

Regularly cleaning your dog's ears will prevent infections.

Those Droopy Eyes

Scenthounds that spend a lot of time with their noses to the ground can be prone to getting foreign objects in their eyes, especially if they spend their days trailing or just snuffling around outside in heavy brush. Bloodhounds in particular have quite a few folds and droops around the eyes and a lower lid that pulls up to protect the eyes against underbrush. Any dog with lots of facial skinfolds needs a little extra attention to the eye area. Moisture and dirt can collect within skinfolds of the eye and become infected. Keep skinfolds around the eyes clean and dry.

but clean as far as you can see. Dogs with long, floppy ears are particularly prone to yeast infections, and pests like fleas and ticks are often visible on the ears, so take a good close look. After cleaning, make sure your dog's ears are thoroughly dry, as moisture can also promote yeast or bacterial infections.

Examine your dog's eyes and wipe away any discharge. If your dog has a white coat and tearstains, you can use a special product made to remove tearstains (usually a cosmetic problem only). Check for irritation, too. Some dogs suffer from entropion, a genetic condition in which the lid turns inward and eyelashes can scratch your dog's cornea. Also check that eyes are clear. Cloudiness could indicate cataracts, so see your vet if you think your dog's eyes look cloudy. Redness and irritation can also indicate a foreign object in the eye. Don't try to remove anything from your dog's eye yourself. See your vet. If your dog has allergies, his eyes could become red and irritated. See your vet if you suspect seasonal allergies.

Next, pull back your dog's lips and get a good look at his teeth. Are they white and shiny, or yellow with plaque? Oral bacteria has been linked to heart disease in dogs, so keeping your dog's teeth clean and plaque-free is essential for good health, especially in senior dogs. Make sure your dog gets to eat something crunchy every day–hard kibble, a crunchy biscuit, or even carrots and pieces of apple if your dog likes them. Also invest in a toothbrush or tooth scrubber that fits over your finger, and toothpaste made just for dogs. Dogs can get sick from eating human toothpaste, but dog toothpaste is edible and tastes like meat so dogs can't resist it. Brush your dog's teeth carefully and remember how important it is that your dog accepts handling of his mouth by you, your vet, and any prospective show dog judges, too.

If your dog's eyes are red or irritated, he may have allergies.

Part 2

Time to clip those nails! Some dogs dislike nail trimming, but handling a dog's feet every day from puppyhood can make nail trimming much easier. See a groomer or your vet to have a very resistant dog's nails trimmed, but the job will be much easier and cheaper if you can do it yourself. First, take a look at your dog's nails. If they are light colored, you can see the quick, a vein that runs about half way down the nail. Dark nails will hide the quick. Begin by snipping off just the tip of your dog's nails with the guillotine-style nail trimmer or grinding them flat with a dremel tool or nail grinder. If you trim your dog's nails every week, they will stay short. If you've waited awhile, you may have to cut off more.

At last, you are ready to brush down that lovely coat. The tools and techniques to use depend on

Don't Clip That Quick!

The more you trim your dog's nails, the farther back the quick will recede, but if you accidentally clip the quick—the vein that runs part way down your dog's nail—your dog's nail will bleed. Apply a styptic pencil or other antiseptic coagulant to the nail. Your dog will not enjoy a clipped quick and could become afraid of nail clipping sessions if he is very sensitive, so avoid this if possible, but don't worry about the blood indicating anything serious. Stop the bleeding, reassure your dog without making a big deal of it, and move on to the next step. If you continue to trim the nails every week without incident, your dog should soon learn that nail clipping doesn't always mean a clipped quick.

your dog's coat type, so read on to determine the best way to groom your dog's crowning glory.

Bathing

Some dogs, such as some scenthounds and those with long coats that spend a lot of time working hard outdoors and getting really dirty, tend to develop odors due to lots of sebaceous glands and/or skinfolds.

Other dogs, such as inside pets with smooth coats and sensitive skin, don't need a bath more than a couple of times a year unless they have an encounter with something stinky, sticky, or extra dirty. But no matter whether you do it often or not often at all, every pet owner should know how to give his or her pup a bath.

First, decide where you will bathe your dog. The bathtub works for most dogs, but close the doors and have plenty of towels ready so your sopping wet pup doesn't escape and go bounding around the house spraying water. Some larger dogs may enjoy an outdoor bath with the garden hose and a big tub or kiddie pool, but make sure the hose water hasn't been sitting in the sun. In other words, don't burn your dog! Test the water first, and never bathe a dog outside if the weather is even a little bit chilly.

Brush and comb out your dog's coat, removing all tangles and mats. If your dog has mats you can't remove, have a groomer try, unless you prefer to clip your dog's coat short. (This can compromise a show-coat's quality, so be sure that's what you really want to do.)

Once the coat is tangle-free, soak your dog thoroughly with lukewarm water to the skin. A hand-held showerhead works

Proper oral hygiene helps keep your dog's mouth healthy.

Some dogs require a bath more often than others.

well. Apply dog shampoo appropriate for your dog's coat and work through with a sponge or your fingers. Brush the shampoo into your dog's coat with bristle brush. Use a small bristle brush around the face to avoid getting shampoo in the eyes. Rinse your dog thoroughly to the skin to remove all the shampoo. Apply conditioner according to the directions and rinse again. Squeeze excess water from your dog's coat with your hands and towel dry thoroughly.

You can use a hair dryer on a cool setting to dry your dog's coat.

Blow-dry long coats and thick or double short coats on low setting while brushing with a bristle brush. Short, wiry, and smooth coats can air-dry. Long coats can get puffy without blow-drying and brushing, which gives them a smooth texture. Blow-dry curly coats according to how you want them to look when dry–talk to your groomer.

Unless you want your wet puppy rolling around joyfully in the mud, keep him inside until he is completely dry.

Coat Types

Dogs may all be members of *canis familiarus* but when it comes to coats, they are about as different as you can imagine. Put a black and tan Manchester Terrier next to a black Miniature Poodle in a full show clip and the difference is clear. Your dog's coat type determines the necessary grooming tools and techniques, and coat types come in five basic types:

1. Longhaired, like the Shih Tzu, Bearded Collie, English Toy Spaniel, and Afghan Hound

2. Shorthaired, like the Labrador Retriever, Rottweiler, Alaskan Malamute, and Norwegian Elkhound

3. Smoothhaired, like the Boxer, Basenji, Whippet, and Great Dane

3. Wirehaired, like the Schnauzer, Airedale, Cairn Terrier, and Wirehaired Pointing Griffon

4. Curly, like the Poodle, Puli, Irish Water Spaniel, and Bedlington Terrier

Let's look at each type and what is required to keep that special coat its most beautiful.

Longhaired Coats

Whether you've got a tiny Maltese or a magnificent Afghan Hound, if you have to groom a longhaired coat, you have some serious work to do. You will probably spend far more time brushing out your dog than anyone whose dog has a different coat type. Let a longhaired coat go unbrushed for more than a week, and you've got an even more prodigious job. A badly matted long coat may indeed be beyond saving, and your only option may be to shave the dog and start over. For this reason, regular brushing at least *every other day* is essential for longhaired breeds and a thorough down-to-the-skin brush and comb-out should be a weekly habit.

Dogs with long coats require extra grooming.

Because brushing and combing a longhaired breed takes so long, it can become an excellent way for you and your pet to spend time together. Brush and comb your little Lhasa Apso or Tibetan Terrier in front of the TV each evening or after the morning walk. Longhaired breeds trained from puppyhood to stand patiently for brushing will be much easier to keep well groomed.

Many owners of dogs with longhaired coats choose to have their pets professionally groomed about once a month because they don't have the time to keep those long lovely coats in perfect condition, but even so, longhaired breeds require regular brushing sessions to maintain the coat between professional groomings.

Others opt to keep their longhaired friends in so-called "puppy clips" or "pet clips" or other shorter styles like Schnauzer trims to make those long coats more practical and easier to manage, not to mention less prone to matting. If you have a longhaired breed because you love that gorgeous coat, you may find the extra work worth it, but if you just love your little puppy because of his sparkling personality, you may really enjoy the convenience of a pet clip.

Mats are not only unsightly. They can hide skin conditions and other problems on a dog, so keep your longhaired friend in good coat. The great thing about brushing a longhaired breed is the end result. A freshly brushed Shih Tzu, Yorkie, Pomeranian, or Chow Chow is a glorious sight and well worth the effort.

Other larger, longhaired breeds such as Samoyeds, Collies, Sheepdogs, and Chow Chows are also sometimes shaved down when they get overly matted or with the change of seasons. These larger breeds take even longer to brush out but are spectacular in their full coats.

Grooming a Longhaired Coat

Brushing a longhaired coat is different than brushing any other kind of coat. If the job looks too tough, consult a professional, but for daily brushing, follow these steps, which also include instructions for a monthly (or more often) shampoo.

Steps for grooming a longhaired dog:

√ Spray coat with coat conditioner to make brushing easier and less damaging to hair.

√ Brush through with pin brush or in the case of a neglected coat, a wire slicker brush.

√ For heavy coats, brush in layers.

Longhaired Coat Grooming Tools

√ Spray coat conditioner

√ Wire slicker brush

√ Pin brush

√ Mat comb

√ Basic comb with a coarse (widely spaced teeth) and fine (narrowly spaced teeth) sides

√ Small scissors

√ Shampoo for long coats

√ Conditioner for long coats

√ Large bristle brush

√ Small bristle brush

√ Blow dryer with low setting

You may choose to get your dog groomed professionally.

√ For the Lhasa Apso, Shih Tzu, Yorkshire Terrier, Silky Terrier, Skye Terrier, Tibetan Terrier, Maltese, and Afghan Hound, make a straight part with a comb down the back and brush coat down either side.

√ Comb through mats with mat comb.

√ Comb hair with coarse side of basic comb.

√ Comb hair with fine side of basic comb.

√ Trim excess hair from around the feet so hair is level with the floor and from between foot pads.

√ Trim hair from inside ears.

√ Tie hair back from face if appropriate (typically for smaller longhaired dogs).

√ Clip nails, clean ears, brush teeth.

√ Bathe approximately monthly and blow-dry/brush coat smooth.

A Pretty Topknot

The Yorkshire Terrier and Shih Tzu traditionally (in the show ring) have their topknots tied with a ribbon, and the Maltese traditionally gets two ribbons, but other longhaired pets like Lhasa Apsos and Afghans also may enjoy the increased vision and you may enjoy the crisp appearance of a ribbon-tied topknot.

Shorthaired Coat Grooming Tools

√ Sturdy natural bristle brush or pin brush

√ Wire slicker brush

√ Small scissors

√ All-purpose shampoo or shampoo appropriate to coat color

√ Coat conditioner or lanolin spray

√ Blow dryer with low setting

Shorthaired Coats

Shorthaired coats are typically short and dense, sometimes with undercoats and sometimes without, and are easy to care for; think Labrador Retriever, Norwegian Elkhound, German Shepherd Dog, and Welsh Corgi. While shorthaired coats are far easier to brush than longhaired coats, they also tend to shed a lot, some all season long and some approximately twice a year, typically in fall and spring. Nordic dogs like Siberian Huskies, Alaskan Malamutes, and other breeds from colder climates tend to have a much thinner coat during warm weather, so spring and summer can be heavy shedding periods.

Grooming a shorthaired coat is a pleasure. A vigorous brushing with a natural bristle brush or pin brush is all it takes, and shorthaired dogs typically really enjoy a good brush-down. During periods of heavier shedding, a wire slicker brush or other brush designed for a shedding dog can help to remove greater quantities of hair. A good weekly brushing during most of the year and a good daily brushing during shedding periods can drastically reduce the amount of shed hair you will find around the house. Keep ear and foot hair trimmed, teeth clean, and nails short, and you're done!

Shorthaired breeds don't need bathing nearly as often as longhaired breeds. Their easy-care coats and the oil glands in their skin keep skin and coat clean. Some shorthaired breeds are so soil-resistant that they can get very dirty, dry out, and all the dirt just falls away on its own or with a little help from a bristle brush. In fact, bathing a shorthaired coat too often can strip the natural oils from coat and skin, making it appear less groomed and less resistant to weather and dirt. Bathe your shorthaired breed two or three times a year, unless he gets into something really smelly or too dirty for the coat to self-clean. Use a coat conditioner or lanolin spray made for lubricating skin and coats after a bath to restore suppleness and sheen that may be stripped from the shampoo. Ask your groomer or knowledgeable pet store retailer for product suggestions.

Smoothhaired coats are the easiest to groom.

If weather is chilly, blow-dry your shorthaired dog's coat after bathing. Dense double coats can take a long time to dry. If you don't mind watching your happy pup roll around on the lawn in his newly washed coat, you can let him dry outdoors on a warm sunny day instead of blow-drying, but he may just get dirty all over again. (Of course, he'll have a lot of fun doing it!)

Smoothhaired Coats

Smoothhaired coats are the easiest to groom. Burnished, glossy, hard, slick, and close, smoothhaired coats are both low-maintenance and gorgeous. Think of a gleaming

Smoothhaired Coat Grooming Tools

√ Natural bristle brush or hound glove with natural bristles

√ Rubber curry comb for large smoothhaired breeds like Boxers, Mastiffs, and Dalmatians

√ All-purpose shampoo or shampoo appropriate to coat color

√ Coat dressing or lanolin spray

√ A square of velvet

The Pug's smooth coat is self-cleaning.

Boxer, a lustrous Doberman, a polished Pug, or a sleek and shiny Whippet. All smoothhaired breeds, from the aerodynamic Greyhound to the sagaciously droopy Bloodhound, should have a sleek and gleaming coat.

Some smoothhaired coats shed a lot, and some barely at all or only seasonally. In either case, all a smoothhaired coat requires is a weekly brushing with a natural bristle brush or a hound glove to keep the coat smooth and characteristically shiny. Dogs with smoothhaired coats tend to have sensitive skin, so bathing is even less necessary for these breeds than for shorthaired breeds. Twice a year is plenty unless, of course, your puppy gets into something that just won't brush out. Choose a gentle shampoo for sensitive skin. Shampoos designed to emphasize black or white coats can make the smoothhaired coat even more stunning. End with a rubdown to help redistribute natural skin oils to the coat. You might also add a quick spritz with a lanolin spray or polish the coat with a square of velvet for truly breathtaking and light-catching results.

Trim nails, polish teeth, and that's it. How simple is that?

For Bloodhounds, Basset Hounds, and Coonhounds, it is especially important to clean ears thoroughly with rubbing alcohol and dry well to prevent odor and infection.

Wirehaired Coats

Some people just adore the whiskery, bearded look of the wirehaired dog. Wirehaired Dachshunds, Schnauzers, German Wirehaired Pointers, Wirehaired Pointing Griffons, and many of the terriers, such as the Cairn, Airedale, Border, Welsh, Lakeland, and of course the Wirehaired Fox Terrier have this unique, coarse wirehaired coat. This weatherproof coat helped farm dogs resist inclement weather conditions and underbrush as they patrolled for vermin.

The wirehaired coat is unique in that it doesn't really shed and instead of regular brushing, it requires a procedure called plucking or stripping. Because of its coarse texture, dead hairs don't fall out of the wirehaired coat. After hairs complete a growth cycle, the dog "blows coat," but unlike fluffier breeds whose soft hair falls out in tufts during a seasonal shed, the wirehaired coat hairs stay put and you or your groomer must pluck them out. If you don't strip a wirehaired coat, it can become tangled and matted, compromising both the dog's appearance and health.

> ## Wirehaired Coat Grooming Tools
> √ Pin brush
>
> √ Stripping knife (optional, if you plan to strip rather than clip your dog)
>
> √ Clippers for trimming and shaping, or for clipping down the entire coat as an alternative to stripping
>
> √ Scissors for neatening
>
> √ All-purpose shampoo or shampoo appropriate for wirehaired coats
>
> √ Conditioner or baby oil to keep dry hairs from breaking

Some people choose to clip down their wirehaired pets, and this is an easy way to manage a wirehaired coat if you don't plan to show your dog. Clipping eventually compromises the course texture. The coat will become softer and less characteristic, but for a pet dog, this may make no difference at all.

For larger wirehaired dogs like the Scottish Deerhound and the Irish Wolfhound, stripping is unnecessary. Brush thoroughly with a pin brush to remove excess hair. Some people like to strip the long hairs on the ears and belly, but the rest of the coat doesn't require it. The large wirehaired herding breeds like the Giant Schnauzer and the Bouvier des Flandres benefit from an all-over stripping, but again, many pet owners choose to clip these breeds as a much simpler alternative to stripping the substantial coat of a large herding dog.

Whether you decide to clip or strip your wirehaired dog, also brush him regularly with a pin brush, which can remove some of the excess hair, and keep that dry haircoat well conditioned or lubricated by rubbing a small amount of mineral oil between your palms and smoothing it over the coat before brushing to prevent hairs from breaking.

Stripping the Wirehaired Coat

Because stripping is a big job, many who wish to maintain the characteristic hard coat take their wirehaired pets to the groomer. If you want to strip your pet yourself, talk to the breeder or your groomer about the individual method most desirable for your pet, since wirehaired breeds are each groomed according to breed, and clipped and scissored into a certain style after bathing and drying. After your dog's outline is in the proper style, you can strip or pluck the coat.

To pluck, work through the entire coat, grasping small tufts of hair and pulling out the dead hairs straight from the roots (don't twist or pull at an angle or hairs will break off). When done correctly, plucking doesn't hurt your dog, and dogs that are plucked here and there every week (called "rolling" a coat, as an alternative to stripping out all dead hairs seasonally) will be accustomed to and enjoy this grooming. You can also use a stripping knife (ask your groomer to show you how), but plucking is fine and easier to do on a regular basis.

Curly Coats

The curly-coated breeds are among the most difficult to groom. Grooming a curly-coated breed in the correct style is a job for a professional. Unless you plan to keep your frizzy friend clipped down (something many pet owners choose for convenience), you *will* want to have your pretty Poodle, corded Puli, powder-puff Bichon, little-lamb Bedlington Terrier, wavy Kerry Blue Terrier, or dreadlocked Komondor professionally groomed.

The Poodle's curly coat is difficult to groom.

If you have an Irish Water Spaniel or American Water Spaniel, you may be able to keep the curly coats of these sporting breeds in line on your own with very frequent, thorough brushing to prevent mats, but even these breeds are more easily groomed professionally, because groomers are experts at removing mats without damaging coats. Mats are a constant problem in curly-coated breeds, especially for working spaniels.

Ask your groomer how you should maintain your dog between professional grooming and be sure to keep your curly buddy's nails trimmed, teeth cleaned, and ears and eyes immaculate. Even pet clips for Poodles and Bichons are best done professionally. It's worth the extra money, and you can spend the time you save playing with your curly pal.

Your Grooming Log

A grooming log is a handy thing to have. In it, you record, in diary-fashion, what you did and what you found. A grooming log is an essential tool for maintaining your dog's health and can be a key factor in helping your vet to diagnose a health problem.

Once you've completed your weekly grooming session, whether it is a brief between-professional-grooming maintenance session or a thorough bath-and-comb grooming marathon, record the results in a grooming log.

Remember the grooming exam described at the beginning of the chapter? Keep your grooming log nearby and record anything unusual you find when examining your dog. Did you notice a little bump just behind your Border Collie's right ear? Did your Golden Retriever flinch when you rubbed her tummy? Did your Westie have a red, itchy spot on his left leg? Keep track of anything unusual.

Also make a general note of your dog's coat condition, skin condition, whether you trimmed his nails, cleaned her ears, mopped up his runny eyes, or clipped away any mats. Note whether you found any evidence of a pest problem. Note any special products you used, like pest control, mineral oil on

Curly-Coated Grooming Tools

See a professional. Really. A curly-coated breed is super tough to groom. If you really want to learn and are prepared for a time-consuming hobby, have a professional give you a few hands-on lessons and be prepared to make some mistakes, which will, luckily, grow out...eventually. Your groomer can also recommend the right tools for your particular pet's curly coat.

Grooming can help you keep on top of any skin problems your dog may have.

Memory Book

The grooming log is an invaluable tool for keeping track of your dog's health status, but it can also serve as a memory book. In addition to basic care information, also jot any funny stories about your pet. Did he do a neat trick today? Steal your sandwich? Curl up with the cat? Carry your underwear into the dining room mid-dinner-party? If you record pet stories in your journal, you may someday cherish it as a lovely and touching way to re-experience memories of your pet after he has passed on.

the coat, petroleum jelly to moisten a dry nose, coat whitener, or canine cologne for beautification. Any future allergy conditions could be traced back to products used in grooming, and you might not remember what you used at a future vet visit.

Finally, make some behavioral notes. How much did your dog eat and drink today (especially if it varied from the norm)? Did she do anything unusual, such as seem uncharacteristically fatigued, unwilling to go on a walk, unusually sensitive to heat or cold, grumpy or snappy or particularly hyperactive?

Every time you visit your vet, bring along your grooming log. Chances are, you'll be amazed at how handy it is to have all that information recorded for future reference. While you're at it, record every vet visit and everything that was done, from vaccinations and tests to prescribed medication.

Part Three

Plan for a Healthy Life

MPIFER
© 2002

"Your temprature is a normal 98 Fahrenheit, Mr. Sparkey.
'Course that's 418 in dog Degrees."

Your Healthy Puppy

This book is all about the big picture–the good life for your dog, which is a combination of good health, emotional well-being, and positive relationships with people. Any dog not suffering from a health problem or genetically predisposed to a bad temperament can enjoy a good life with the right humans to take care of him, and even those that seem to be without hope can sometimes overcome the odds. In fact, over the years I've heard plenty of stories about dogs with seemingly little potential–canine street urchins, slaves to dog-fighting rings, hopeless cases returned to shelters over and over–finally blossoming into ideal pets, even heroes, under the care of the right owner.

All puppies have the potential to be great pets.

A physically and mentally healthy dog will have a long and happy life.

The sad fact is, however, that most dogs that start out unsocialized, untrained, and without proper veterinary care, not to mention those thousands of dogs who are a product of bad breeding in the first place, don't end up heroes or even cherished pets. Most of these dogs end up sick, in trouble, in the animal shelter, or worse.

That doesn't mean you shouldn't help out a down-on-his-luck pup! I did it myself, and I commend anyone else who does it. Later in this chapter we'll talk about the best way to go about adopting a dog from a shelter or rescue group. But (and this is very important!), life with a sick or temperamentally difficult dog, let alone a great dog who just doesn't match your individual needs, is incredibly stressful and even the most well intentioned have been known to throw in the towel…and throw out the dog.

The good news is that with a little careful planning, common sense, and some specific knowledge, you can find a puppy or adult dog that is healthy–physically, emotionally,

Your Social Butterfly

Socialization, as used in this book, is the process of introducing positive associations to your puppy via many different stimuli so that your puppy learns from the beginning that people, places, and distractions are generally good, rather than something to be feared or attacked. Young puppies should meet many different people of all ages, genders, sizes, colors, and shapes, as well as other dogs, and other pets. They should be exposed to many different situations, from parking lots and the outsides of stores with automatic doors to dog parks, soccer games, and the neighborhood. Socialization teaches puppies to be good citizens with even temperaments, but it *will not erase protective instincts* in dogs that are naturally protective. Socializing your dog will not take away his ability to be a good guard dog. Instead, it will teach him the subtleties of life so that he will be more equipped to tell good from bad, friend from intruder.

socially. You can find a dog that will make your life better, not worse; a dog with whom you can forge a lasting, loving, and mutually beneficial relationship. You can find a dog like this almost anywhere, as long as you know what to look for, and what to avoid.

A good beginning for a happy, healthy puppy comes from good breeding, proper health care, thorough socialization, bonding with you, and lots of fun and friendly training. The best place to start, of course, is with a healthy puppy. This chapter will help you to find a healthy puppy with great potential, and will help you to put into place those health and behavior habits that will last you and your dog a lifetime.

Choosing a Healthy Puppy

Where do you find a healthy puppy? Considering that every year in the US, more dogs are born than humans, healthy puppies are everywhere. Unfortunately, so are unhealthy, badly bred, unsocialized puppies.

Finding a healthy puppy isn't just a matter of getting lucky. How do you know you are choosing a puppy with great health? The best way is to know exactly where your puppy came from, and there are several ways to get this crucial information. One is by buying your puppy from a quality breeder who can not only tell you but show you exactly where your puppy came from by letting you meet the puppy's parents and even other relatives like uncles, aunts, and grandparents. They will also be able to provide records of health tests and vaccinations, and hold frank discussions about what they do to socialize their puppies.

The more you know about your puppy's origins, the better equipped you are to care for him.

Another option is to find a puppy at a shelter or from a rescue group that carefully monitors and tests the dogs that are relinquished. Some families have to give up their pets due to reasons they can't help and provide full information on the dog's past. Many dogs in shelters and with rescue groups are given full

What About That Doggy in the Window?

Although the puppy in the pet store may look absolutely irresistible, pet stores may not be the best place to buy puppies. You can't normally see the parents of a pet-shop puppy, and pet-store retailers don't usually have the time or the qualifications for monitoring puppy health and temperament. Your chances for finding a healthy puppy of a breed that is right for you are much better if you adopt from a rescue group or buy from a quality breeder. If you can't resist that pet-shop puppy, make sure to take your new pet to the vet on the way home from the pet store for a thorough health checkup. Of course, you were going to do that anyway, right?

and thorough veterinary examinations and behavior tests, and are neutered if necessary. Shelter and rescue workers are also often very experienced and good at analyzing a dog's temperament and tendencies, although pet overpopulation has pushed many groups beyond their capacity. They are so crowded that workers are not able to spend as much time as would be ideal in monitoring the dogs that come through the system.

You can do certain tests and make certain observations on your own, too, although whenever getting a dog from a shelter or rescue group, you can never know firsthand what has happened in that dog's past. You could have some surprises in store–pleasant or unpleasant. My dog, a Rat Terrier from the local animal shelter, is the most well-behaved dog I've ever had. Other dogs from shelters can seem friendly at first, but may later prove to be unpredictable.

Of course, simply buying from a breeder doesn't guarantee that you'll get a healthy dog. First, find a quality breeder whose ideals match yours, who is knowledgeable and communicative, and whom you feel you can trust. Do your own research, too, so you aren't completely at the breeder's mercy for information. Knowing what makes a breeder good and what red flags may signal a less-than-quality breeder can help you to find the breeder that is right for you.

Finding a Breeder

Lots of people breed dogs, and most people who have never bought a dog from a breeder before (and some who have) don't have any idea what makes a good breeder. The first dog

I ever bought was obviously from a horrible backyard breeder who was not socializing or taking very good care of her dogs, but I didn't know any better. I thought all breeders' facilities looked like that–crowded rows of small wire kennels filled with oversized Miniature Pinschers yapping hysterically, puppies missing patches of hair, and a general air of chaos and filth–because I had never seen anything different. If only I had known then what I know now, after years of meeting and interviewing breeders and seeing the good, the bad, and the downright ugly, I would have run in the opposite direction! (That Miniature Pinscher was timid, a fear biter, and had epilepsy, by the way.)

Work with a breeder that is dedicated to improving the breed.

Because of the Internet, potential pet owners now have access to hundreds of breeders, so even if you are set on a Papillion or a Beauceron or a Catahoula Leopard Dog and nobody is breeding them in your area, you can probably get one.

But having access to breeders all over the country, even the world, makes screening breeders for quality and responsibility even more difficult. Even so, I've discovered that there are certain qualities really good breeders generally have in common and certain red flags that often indicate a sub-standard breeder. Some of these you can find out about through email or phone communication, but in most cases, you should take a trip and visit the breeder in person. Really particular breeders will usually make you do this anyway, although there are exceptions. Maybe the breeder that has your perfect puppy really does breed three different breeds of dogs really, really well and will ship to you from her in-home operation in Fairbanks, or maybe the breeder who seemed so smart and caring and diligent will turn out to be anything but.

In general, however, looking out for the qualities on the "Good Breeder" list and steering clear of the qualities on the "Not-So-Good" Breeder list can help you make a more informed decision about the breeder who is right for you.

Part 3

Breeder Knows Best

What if you spend a lot of time with a breeder, and then she refuses to sell you a puppy? This happens frequently with responsible breeders who won't sell puppies to homes that they don't believe are suited for their precious charges. Maybe you have boisterous children too young to safely handle a delicate Pomeranian puppy. Maybe you don't have a fence and the breeder knows that Siberian Husky will be long gone within a matter of weeks. Maybe you work all day and your needy Whippet will shiver away to nothing without human companionship. Most of the time, the breeder is only acting in the dog's best interest. She just may be saving you from lots of heartache and trouble. Rather than getting angry, talk frankly with the breeder about why she doesn't think you should own one of her puppies, and ask her what breed she thinks might suit your needs better. A boisterous Lab puppy loves to play with boisterous kids. A toy dog can get plenty of exercise indoors and doesn't necessarily need a fenced yard. A Basset Hound may be perfectly happy to snooze all day when you are at work, as long as you pay him lots of attention when you get home. Just because this particular breeder doesn't have a dog to suit your needs doesn't mean there isn't a perfect dog out there just waiting for you to find him.

The puppy you choose should be outgoing and healthy looking.

The Good Breeder List

You're on your way to visit the breeder of the puppy you hope you will bring home with you. But how do you know that breeder is doing a good job? Check for the following qualities, answers, and conditions in your breeder and her facility. If the breeder you visit measures up to this criteria, you've probably got a gem. Start getting to know those puppies!

√ First impressions first. The breeder is friendly, open, and gives the impression of honesty. Sure, some people can seem friendly and honest even if they aren't, but listen to your gut. Do you trust this person?

√ The breeder seems to know a lot about the breed. Ask questions about the breed's temperament, health issues, energy level, and history, even if you already know. The breeder should know at least as much as you do about the breed, and ideally will know much more from her years of experience.

Part 3

√ In addition to the good qualities of the breed, the breeder also tells you all the challenges and down sides to the breed in order to fully prepare you for the commitment ahead.

√ The breeder breeds only one or possibly two similar breeds.

√ The breeder has been in the business for many years or, if just starting, is working closely with experienced breeders with good reputations.

√ The breeder shows you evidence of health tests performed on the parents of the litter, such as hips and elbows certified free of dysplasia through the Orthopedic Foundation for Animals (OFA) and eyes certified free of progressive retinal atrophy through the Canine Eye Registration Foundation (CERF). If your breed has the gene for piebald coloration (large patches of two or more colors, usually including white), such as a Dalmatian, Bull Terrier, Beagle, or English Setter, ask the breeder whether she has had the puppies brainstem auditory evoked response (BAER) tested for deafness.

√ The breeder is happy to give you the number of her vet and other references. (Check them!)

√ The breeder grills you about where you live, whether you have children, whether you have a fence, why you want this particular breed, whether you've raised a puppy before, and other questions you might consider none of her business. That means the breeder cares about where her puppies will go and doesn't want to put them in a bad situation. That's a great quality in a breeder, so don't be offended.

√ The breeder raises the puppies in the house where they can be in frequent contact with humans. (Some large breeds and working breeds actually prefer life outdoors, but puppies should at least be given in-the-house time every day.)

The breeder will supply the name of her vet along with other references.

Part 3

A breeder's contract should ensure the health of your puppy.

√ The breeder is already familiar with the different personalities and tendencies of the individual puppies in the litter.

√ The breeder holds and plays with the puppies every day to help socialize them, starting soon after birth.

√ The whelping area is clean and smells pleasant.

√ The breeder is happy to introduce you to the mother of the litter, and maybe even the father (although many sires don't live with the breeder).

√ The mother of the litter is friendly and looks healthy.

√ The puppies look plump and clean, with no crusted feces on their rears, no runny eyes or noses, no parasites, and no missing patches of hair. They are energetic and curious.

√ The breeder refuses to sell you a puppy younger than eight weeks old. (Some toy breeds shouldn't leave the whelping box until 12 weeks.)

√ The breeder requires that you both sign a contract guaranteeing the puppy's health for a certain period of time under the condition that you take the puppy immediately to a vet for a checkup.

√ The breeder's contract also requires you to promise you will return the dog to the breeder if you are ever unable to keep it, for any reason at any time (but not for a refund of money unless the reason for the return is the fault of the breeder, such as a serious genetic fault or contagious disease the puppy contracted while in the care of the breeder).

√ The contract also requires that you neuter your pet, and the breeder requires proof that you have done so. If you buy a show dog and plan to exhibit your prized pet in the conformation show ring, the breeder will not require that you neuter your dog, as this would disqualify him from the ring. However, in this case, the breeder may require or

Part 3

request that any future mating be done under her guidance or may ask for the privilege of picking a puppy from any future litter.

√ The breeder requests that you use her as a resource for information in the future (within reason–don't call her at all hours asking questions you can easily find answers to in dog care books or from your vet). Breeders can be an invaluable and lifelong source of information and guidance, and they usually love to keep in touch with their puppies as they grow.

How did your breeder do? Pretty well or not so well? If you have doubts about your breeder (or even if you don't think you have doubts), also see how your potential puppy's first human companion measures up against the Not-So-Good Breeder list.

The Not-So-Good Breeder List

You're not quite sure this breeder is breeding with your puppy's good health and sound temperament in mind. Be sure–and run the other way fast without looking any further at the puppies–if the breeder you are visiting has any of the following qualities:

√ First impressions first. The breeder is hurried, seems suspicious, acts like you are wasting her time, or doesn't give the impression of honesty. Use your instincts. If you don't feel like the breeder is trustworthy or you get the impression she is hiding something, thank her and move on.

The Price of a Good Dog

"What—$500 for a Labrador Retriever? When they're "Free to Good Home" in that box in front of the Mini-Mart?" Those who aren't familiar with the world of purebred dogs can sometimes be shocked by a puppy's price tag, but $500 (prices on purebred dogs vary according to breed and geographical location) for a healthy, well-bred puppy from a quality breeder is actually a small price to pay. The money you will probably save on vet bills, not to mention liability, is well worth starting out with a good puppy. Don't think the breeder is laughing all the way to the bank, either. Good dog breeders don't make money at breeding dogs. Ethical, responsible breeding is incredibly expensive, and quality breeders do it for the love of the dogs, not the money. Consider what your $500 is buying you: great genetics, the chance to meet the parents and see what great dogs they are, a health guarantee, superb socialization from the beginning, and the breeder herself, who can be a lifelong contact and source of information and help, not to mention someone who loves your puppy so much that she will take him back any time, for any reason, if you can't keep him. Consider it a steal.

Part 3

√ The breeder doesn't seem to know much about the breed or only tells you the good things. Every breed has its down side, and breeders who don't let you know the challenges may just be trying to make a quick buck. If you know more about the breed than the breeder, move on.

√ The breeder breeds many different breeds and/or runs a huge breeding operation with many rows of kennels.

√ The breeder never allows the puppies in the house. (There are exceptions and if this is the only item on this list that applies to your breeder, use your good judgment.)

√ The breeder is just breeding her first or second litter and doesn't know any of the experienced breeders in the business. Ask where she got the dam and sire and how she decided to start breeding. "I thought it would be fun" is not a good answer.

√ The breeder tells you that health tests in this breed aren't necessary or doesn't appear to know anything about health tests.

√ The breeder is reluctant to give you the number of her vet and other references, or says she never takes her puppies to the vet because "they are so healthy."

√ The breeder doesn't ask you anything about how you live, where you will keep the dog, or your dog experience. She seems more concerned with convincing you to buy a puppy, not with whether you would make a good guardian for this breed and this puppy.

√ The breeder tries to get you to buy a puppy that is sick or shy.

√ The breeder doesn't know anything about the individual puppies in the litter or says they are "all about the same."

√ The breeder doesn't frequently hold or play with or otherwise socialize the puppies, or doesn't seem to know anything about puppy socialization. (Ask what she does to socialize the puppies.)

√ The whelping area is dirty and smells bad. Puppies defecate often so an occasional pile or puddle is normal, but you should get the impression the whelping area is cleaned and sterilized frequently (that means daily).

√ The breeder makes excuses for why you can't see either of the parents of the litter.

√ The breeder lets you see one or both parents of the litter, but the parents don't match the breed standard in some obvious way (much too big, too small, the wrong color, etc.), look unhealthy, and/or act very shy, aggressive, or unfriendly.

√ The puppies look dirty, skinny, have dull coats, are crusted with feces or dirt, and/or have runny eyes, noses, ears, or missing patches of hair.

√ The puppies have fleas and/or ticks.

√ The puppies are shy, act sleepy all the time (every puppy has to sleep sometimes, but if you catch the litter sleeping, ask when you can come back to see them awake), seem low on energy, and/or are not curious at all to see you or explore their surroundings.

√ The breeder is willing to sell you a puppy younger than eight weeks old.

√ The breeder tries to give you a "deal" on a sick or low-energy puppy.

√ The breeder doesn't require that you sign any kind of contract.

√ The breeder doesn't even mention spaying/neutering a pet.

√ The breeder tells you or gives you the impression that once she has your money, you are on your own.

√ The breeder has a health guarantee that covers the puppy only for a very short period of time, such as 36 hours, after which any further health problems, genetic or not, contracted from the breeder's facility or not, are your problem.

√ You get a bad feeling–trust your instincts.

Let's hope the breeder you find with the puppy you love is a far cry from this last list. Either way, now you know what to expect, what to look for, and how to find a breeder who is doing everything she can to improve the breed and produce healthy, beautiful, and good-tempered puppies.

Second-Hand Dogs

Maybe you are one of those people who, as much as you love dogs and appreciate the qualities of different breeds, doesn't feel the need to have a purebred dog. Maybe you'd rather rescue a mixed breed from the shelter. Or, maybe you have a special affinity for a particular breed, but would rather rescue a dog who has lost her home than buy a puppy from a breeder.

Good for you!

> ### Rescue Me
>
> The AKC keeps a list of purebred dog rescue organizations by breed on their website. Check it out at http://www.akc.org/breeds/rescue.cfm.

There are many advantages to adopting or rescuing a dog.

Second-hand dogs can be the most rewarding of pets. Some people claim (I'm one of them) that dogs from animal shelters seem particularly grateful, as if they understand what you have done for them. Dogs from purebred rescue groups are often well trained and well behaved, but their owners simply couldn't keep them, or they have imperfect conformation but make perfect pets.

There are many other advantages to adopting a second-hand dog:

• Puppies are difficult! Second-hand dogs are usually past the young puppy stage, are already housetrained, and don't have to go out so often. They are past the teething, chewing, and play-biting stages. No puppy whining in the middle of the night, no puppy accidents, no puppy destruction.

• Second-hand dogs are often already familiar with basic obedience commands like "sit," "stay," and "come." It can be fun figuring out what your new dog already knows how to do.

• Second-hand dogs older than age two or three (depending on the breed) are also past the trying stage of canine adolescence (can you say "teenager"?) and have already calmed down considerably.

• Many illnesses and genetic conditions will already have manifested by the time a dog becomes an adult, so if your secondhand dog is healthy, he has a good chance of remaining healthy (provided you take good care of him).

The health and temperament of an older dog is easily determined.

• Second-hand adult dogs cost less initially, have usually already had all their initial puppy vaccinations, are probably already neutered, and don't require puppy supplies. Of course, she will still need regular veterinary checkups, a quality food, and other pet supplies (check out the list later in this chapter for what supplies your dog needs).

• What you see is what you get. An older dog's looks and temperament are pretty much set, unlike with a puppy, where you can never be sure exactly how he will look or act as an adult.

Adoption Nation

According to the 2001-2002 American Pet Products Manufacturers Association (APPMA) National Pet Owners Survey, 20 percent of dogs owned in the US were adopted from animal shelters.

• If you get a puppy from a shelter or rescue group—dogs often come in pregnant and give birth right there in the shelter, or a litter of puppies is abandoned—you can rescue a dog and still start from square one, socializing, training, and bonding with your puppy from the beginning.

Every animal shelter and every rescue group is different. Some have stringent requirements for adopters, such as refusing to allow college students to adopt a dog under any circumstances, no matter how responsible you tell them you are (college students are notorious for abandoning dogs at graduation or during the summer). Some require written permission from a landlord for renters or proof of home ownership, proof of a fence, and detailed personal interviews.

All of this fuss is important, even if you find it irritating. So many dogs are relinquished to shelters and rescue groups each year and so many dogs are returned to shelters and rescue groups that shelter and rescue groups do everything their resources allow them to do in order to stop the cycle of abandonment for each dog they place. They want to be sure that dog has a permanent, loving home. They love dogs and they *don't* want to see your pal back in the shelter again.

So take a deep breath, roll up your pant legs, and wade into the red tape. Your secondhand dog will be well worth it. (I know mine was!)

Signs of Puppy Health

Once you've secured a source for your new puppy, whether breeder, rescue group, or shelter, make sure the pup you choose is as healthy as possible. How do you know? The most important thing for any new puppy owner to do is to take that new puppy immediately to the vet, even before you take it home. Most breeders, shelters, and pet stores require or strongly recommend this practice, and if a vet finds a problem, you can take the puppy back before you ever get it home (if you can bear it—some people would rather pay to fix the problem). The worst-case scenario is a puppy with a serious contagious illness like parvo. In a few cases, puppies won't survive. The pet store, rescue group, shelter, or breeder must know when this happens, and should be willing to reimburse you for any expenses and for the price of the puppy if the problem was already present when you adopted your pup.

Your puppy should display energy and exuberance.

Your vet is the most qualified to assess your new puppy's health, but there are some general signs that a puppy is healthy, and some signs that she isn't. Also look for signs that she has a good temperament. Take this list with you and assess your potential puppy for all of the following:

√ How is his coat? A puppy's coat should be soft, shiny, unmatted, and clean. It shouldn't have any bare patches or look sparse, greasy, or otherwise unhealthy or unkempt.

√ How is the skin beneath the coat? A puppy's skin should be free of red, itchy hot spots and dry flaky patches. Also check for signs of fleas–little black specks of flea dirt or the tiny brown, hopping fleas themselves– and ticks, which can be the size of a pinhead or swollen up to the size of a large beetle, crawling or attached to the skin. Healthy puppy skin should be soft and pinkish.

√ Is your puppy clean? He should not smell badly and should not have any crusted feces, dirt, or discharge from any orifice.

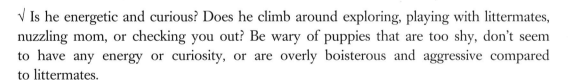

A healthy puppy will be curious about the world around him.

√ Are his eyes bright and shiny without being runny? Is his expression alert?

√ Is he energetic and curious? Does he climb around exploring, playing with littermates, nuzzling mom, or checking you out? Be wary of puppies that are too shy, don't seem to have any energy or curiosity, or are overly boisterous and aggressive compared to littermates.

√ Are his ears clean?

√ Are his teeth white and sharp? (He may not have all his teeth yet, depending on how old he is when you are first introduced.)

√ Is his nose soft and wet without being runny?

√ Are his paws clean and his paw pads soft (not cracked, covered in sores, or dirty)?

√ Is he interested in you? Does he display affection to you? A playful spirit?

If your puppy checks out, let the vet do a more thorough checkup. Once you've got the green light from your vet, you can take that puppy home and begin some serious bonding.

Veterinary Care

Your vet is one of your most important allies in your quest to give your new dog a healthy life. Your vet should see your new puppy several times during the first year for vaccinations and checkups. She can also serve as a resource for information about diet, pest control, grooming, potential emergencies ("My puppy just ate a button—is it an emergency?"), and even basic behavioral modification and training.

But just as it is with medical doctors for humans, some vets have a great rapport with pets and humans alike, and some, even if they are very skilled, may not make you feel comfortable. Having a good relationship with your vet is important. Ideally, you and your vet will understand each other and share a similar philosophy of pet care, whether that means integrating holistic and/or preventive health care measures, sticking to conventional care only, or doing as much as possible on your own at home. When you and your vet are on the same page, everybody wins.

It is important that you choose the best health care for your puppy.

Vet in Training

Do you know where your vet was trained? Many vets post their diplomas on the wall of their offices or clinics, but not all do. Ask your vet where he was trained, and then do a little research on your own. Is the vet school a reputable one? Also ask what his specialty is, what special training he has, and to explain to you his philosophy of pet care. The answers could help you determine whether this is the right vet for you and your dog.

Don't Forget the Annual Checkup

After that first year, you may believe your bouncing adolescent is the picture of perfect health, but don't neglect an annual checkup. The annual exam gives your vet a chance to monitor your dog and could catch a problem before it gets too serious and is still treatable. Of course, if your pet's behavior or habits suddenly change, or if he develops any lumps, bumps, sores, or injuries between annual exams, take him to the vet immediately.

The vet you choose should be familiar with your breed.

Part 3

Choosing a Vet

Choosing a vet is as important as choosing a doctor. In fact, it is choosing a doctor. One nice thing about choosing a vet is that you aren't limited to some insurance company's short list. You can choose anyone you and your dog like.

Schedule appointments to meet a few vets in your area, either just to talk or to have your dog generally checked over for good health. While you are there, pay attention and ask questions. Here's what to look for and what to ask:

√ Is the vet easily accessible? A better vet may be worth a longer drive, but if the vet is too far away and you have an emergency, you may not be able to get there in time. Ask if there is an alternate location for an emergency clinic.

√ Is it easy to make an appointment when you call ahead? Is the receptionist friendly? Will they let you meet the vet and/or schedule a physical for your dog without extra tests? A vet with no time to meet and spend time with potential clients may be too busy when you need her most. On the other hand, a busy vet can be a sign of a quality vet because word gets around.

√ What is your first impression of the reception area? Is it clean and does it smell pleasant? Is the staff friendly and welcoming? Do you feel comfortable there? Bad smells, harried staff, and dirty facilities are all bad signs. Worried animals in the waiting room are, of course, a fixture at any vet.

√ Do you have to wait more than 15 minutes, and if you do, are you told that this is due to unusual circumstances? You and your pet shouldn't be kept waiting for too long. Sure, the vet is busy, but so are you. You don't want a vet who overschedules on purpose.

√ Is the office a large multi-vet practice or a small in-home operation? Which environment do you prefer? Which makes you feel more comfortable?

√ When you are shown into the waiting room, are you made to feel comfortable? Does the staff seem competent? Do they weigh your dog, get him ready, and behave in a professional way that keeps your dog as calm as possible?

√ How does the vet treat you? How does the vet treat your dog? Does she have a friendly,

Fearless Fido?

Your first impression and intuition about a vet can tell you a lot about whether that person will be a good vet for you and your dog. However, don't necessarily take your dog's cue. Many pets are frightened at any veterinarian office, especially those who have had previous unpleasant experiences there (and what puppy enjoys those vaccinations?), or those who are intimidated or riled up by other pets in the waiting room. A frightened puppy isn't necessarily telling you he doesn't like the vet. On the other hand, if you know your dog well and you know he is usually fine with vets but acts strange, either fearful or aggressive, with a particular vet, consider that a red flag.

open personality, or does she seem disinclined to talk to you? Does she act like she likes animals, or does she act like she's burned out and could care less if she ever sees another puppy? Does she act like she loves dogs but can't stand people? A good vet should be able to relate well and communicate well with both you and your dog.

√ After all is said and done, how are the prices? Call around to see if they are comparable to other vets in the area. Prices for veterinary services vary widely according to geographical location, so a vet in Manhattan will probably charge much more than a vet in rural Iowa. A vet in town will probably cost more than a vet outside of town, and may be less crowded–but of course, depending on where you live, you'll have a longer drive.

First Exam

Whether you are still trying out potential vets or have secured one you love, your new puppy must visit the vet right away, preferably on the way home from the breeder, animal shelter, or pet store. At this very first exam, you can expect the vet to do certain things. Although some vets vary according to what they believe is necessary, most vets will begin by checking your new puppy out carefully for genetic defects in structure. The vet will look at and palpate (feel) your puppy's head, ears, eyes, nose, mouth, jaw, neck, spine, legs, tail, genitalia, ribs, and coat for lumps, bumps, or anything malformed. Your vet isn't looking for things that would disqualify a puppy from the show ring, just things that would compromise his health, such as malformed bones, teeth, eyes, or paws; parasites like fleas and ticks; signs of other skin problems such as allergies or fungus; as well as other signs of disease.

Your vet will do a thorough exam of your puppy on his first visit.

If your puppy hasn't yet had his first vaccinations, the vet will administer those, along with a worming, for which you will need a fresh stool sample, so come prepared (see the list provided).

Many vets will also be willing to answer any questions you have about puppy care and may advise you on when to have your pet neutered.

A crate is handy to transport your puppy to and from the vet's office.

Don't come to that first vet visit empty handed. Be sure to bring:

• Your puppy's vaccination history, if he has one.

• Copies of all records of previous medical care for your puppy's file (keep your own copies at home in a safe place, too). If you bought your puppy from a breeder, the breeder should provide you with this information.

• If your puppy is on any medications, even an over-the-counter cream or pet vitamins, bring those in to show your vet.

• That fresh stool sample—collect your puppy's most recent in a plastic bag and keep it in the refrigerator until it's time to go to the vet (you may want to double bag it).

• A list of any questions you will want to remember to ask.

Early Neutering

Some vets and animal shelters now recommend that puppies be neutered much earlier than once recommended because of the benefits to the pets and the owners, and to help stem the pet overpopulation problem. The traditional age for neutering is between six and seven months of age, but some puppies are now neutered as young as six or seven weeks old. While it was once believed that early neutering could compromise growth and other development, the evidence for this is controversial. Studies by the American Veterinary Medical Association (AVMA) show that younger puppies (and kittens) tolerate anesthesia better, recover faster, and make better surgical patients because less abdominal fat makes the surgery easier and faster and the organs more accessible. Later health benefits are the same as for traditional neutering, but because early neutering can be done before owners take home puppies from shelters or breeders, problems with spay/neuter contract compliance can be eliminated. The AVMA now suggests that vets join animal shelters (the first proponents of early neutering) in recommending early neutering.

Vaccinations

When a puppy is nursing, it receives antibodies against disease from its mother's milk (just like a human baby does). Once it stops nursing, however, that protection quickly fades, leaving a new puppy vulnerable to disease. For this reason, newly weaned puppies must begin a vaccination schedule.

Some vets suggest schedules slightly different from this one, and you should follow your vet's recommendation for your individual dog. The following schedule gives you a general idea of what to expect for vaccinations in your puppy's first year.

Vaccinations work on your dog's immune system, activating it against certain infectious conditions by exposing it to tiny bits of the virus that the immune system can handle.

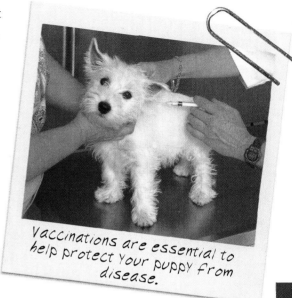

Vaccinations are essential to help protect your puppy from disease.

The typical diseases against which dogs are usually vaccinated include:

- Canine distemper

- Infectious hepatitis

- Canine parvovirus

- Rabies

- Canine parainfluenza

- Bordatella

And, depending on where you live and your dog's risk of exposure:

- Leptospirosis (this vaccine is responsible for 70 percent of post-vaccination

Vaccination Schedule

Puppy's Age	Appropriate Vaccination	Comments
5-6 weeks	First combination vaccine containing: DHPP (distemper, hepatitis, parainfluenza, and parvovirus combined) optional: leptospirosis optional: coronavirus optional: Bordatella optional: Lyme disease	This combination vaccine, sometimes called a 4-way or DHPP (distemper, hepatitis, parainfluenza, parvovirus), or 5-, 6-, or 7-way vaccine if other components are added, varies somewhat according to your vet's opinion about what is necessary and the risk factors in your area. Leptospirosis is rare and the vaccine itself can cause a reaction, so many vets leave it out unless a puppy is at risk. Coronavirus and Lyme disease are also only a concern in certain areas. Your vet can tell you if these are necessary.
8-12 weeks	A second DHPP with other components as recommended	See above
12 weeks	Rabies	Although state laws vary, most states require that pets have a rabies vaccine and a tag to prove it by six months of age.
16 weeks	Third DHPP with other components as recommended	
12–16 months (as vet recommends)	First rabies booster with other components as recommended	Booster vaccines begin in the second year and should be repeated on a schedule recommended by your vet and, in the case of rabies, as required by law (typically every 1 to 3 years)

Part 3

anaphylactic shock reactions and doesn't protect against the two most common strains infecting dogs, so many vets skip this vaccine)

• Coronavirus

• Lyme disease

Unfortunately, not all infectious diseases have vaccines to prevent them or lessen their severity. However, the most common and most dangerous infectious diseases have vaccines, which is why vaccinating your dog is so important.

Once the first year of vaccinations is over, your dog must have booster shots to sustain immunity against infectious diseases. However, vets debate how often booster shots should be administered. The current practice is to revaccinate for most infectious diseases every year, and depending on state law and vaccines used, every one to three years for rabies vaccines. (Your vet will tell you when your dog's next rabies vaccine is required.) But this could be, quite literally, overkill.

Because of vaccinations to pets, many major diseases like distemper–once the number-one killer of dogs–have been virtually eliminated. Now that animals are at a lower risk for contracting certain diseases, vets are able to look more closely at those animals that suffer adverse reactions to vaccinations, either from immediate shock or other acute immune responses to long-term chronic immune system breakdown. Some vets recommend that instead of an annual vaccination, pets should receive an annual blood test that can measure the titer or level of antibodies to diseases in your dog's blood. If your dog has a low titer to any particular disease, he can then be vaccinated for that disease only. In some pets, the first year of vaccinations may take care of immunity for a lifetime, or more typically for two to three years, making annual boosters unnecessary.

Your dog must have regular booster shots to stay healthy.

Vaccination Information

Vaccines come in three types: modified live virus (MLV) vaccines, the most effective and longest lasting because they use the actual live virus to stimulate immunity; inactivated or killed virus, the safest but less effective form of vaccine that uses killed virus cells to stimulate immunity; and recombinant vaccines, a new type of vaccine that uses spliced DNA fragments from a virus. Recombinant vaccines may become the next new wave of vaccines, as they are thought to be as effective as MLVs but without the risk of vaccine reactions, so they may be safer. However, because they are so new, scientists are still waiting to observe the long-term effects.

Studies show that for some diseases in particular, like distemper and canine parvovirus, shots may keep your dog protected up to three years, while immunity from vaccines for other diseases like bordatella and parainfluenza may last less than one year. These effects also vary according to your individual pet, as does sensitivity to vaccines. Talk to your vet about a vaccination schedule that is right for your dog, and consider titer tests, which can definitively determine whether immunity for certain diseases needs a boost or whether your dog is still protected. While you will have to pay for these tests, they could also prevent your dog from unnecessary vaccinations and their possible reactions.

Some sensitive dogs may react badly to certain vaccinations. Anaphylactic shock is a life-threatening reaction that most often occurs in response to the leptospirosis vaccine, but vaccinations can cause other reactions in your dog, from a localized rash and swelling at the vaccination site to unusual but possibly severe reactions like postvaccination encephalitis. Vaccinations are only approved for healthy dogs, so if your dog is in ill health, talk to your vet about the safety of vaccinations and to help you determine which is higher: the risk of your particular dog contracting certain infectious diseases, or the risk of reacting to the vaccination itself.

Supplies

You've found the breeder, the shelter, or the rescue group. You've found the puppy. You've found the vet. What's next?

Shopping!

For those of you who like to shop, this is one of the really fun puppy preparation steps: puppy supplies! Even if you adopt an older dog, you will need certain supplies to keep her happy, healthy, and busy. Take this list to the pet store or to your computer (you can order just about any pet supply online these days), break out that credit card, and have some fun.

And by the way, if you like your furniture, if you want to keep your baseboards, if you would prefer shoes without teeth marks, then puppy toys are *not* an option–they are a necessity.

• Every puppy needs a kennel or crate to use as a den, to escape from the chaos of humans, and to help with housetraining. The crate should be big enough for your puppy to stand up, turn around, and lie down comfortably but not so big that he can soil one side and sleep on the other side. Plastic crates offer a comforting den-like environment, but wire crates work too if you cover part of them with a blanket. Foldaway Pet Carriers by Nylabone® conveniently fold up for easy storage when you're not using them.

• A comfortable, adjustable buckle collar in nylon or leather.

• Other training collars, at the advice of your obedience instructor.

• A 4- or 6-foot leash in leather or nylon.

• An identification tag that includes your phone number.

• A high-quality puppy or dog food. Talk to your vet about what brand he recommends.

• Food and water bowls. For large dogs, consider elevated bowls, which are easier to use. Ceramic and metal bowls are easier to keep clean and germ-free than plastic.

A crate can give your puppy a place to retreat and relax.

Having the right grooming tools helps to keep your puppy looking good.

Part 3

Chew toys help keep your pup occupied and out of mischief.

• Nail clippers made for dogs (don't use the kind made for people).

• Toothbrush and toothpaste made for dogs to keep doggy breath sweet smelling and your dog's teeth tartar free. Dental infections can cause serious health problems in dogs–bacteria can even travel from teeth straight to your dog's heart.

• A brush, flea comb, slicker brush, hound mitt, and/or other appropriate coat care tools for your breed. Talk to your vet, breeder, or groomer about the best way to care for your particular puppy's coat.

• Chew toys. Puppies need to chew, and some dogs continue to require chewing outlets for much of their lives. Try different kinds of chew toys to see what your puppy enjoys. A toy you can fill with peanut butter, treats, and/or kibble, such as a Rhino® by Nylabone®, will keep a boisterous chewer occupied for hours.

• Interactive toys. Your dog loves to do things with you. Interactive toys like pull ropes and items you can throw and your dog can retrieve like balls and Frisbees™ are important for maintaining your relationship.

• Pest control, if necessary. The easiest to use and probably the most effective are those spot-on treatments that you apply between your dog's shoulder blades once every month, like Advantage™ and Frontline™. These are best purchased through your vet.

And for those of you who have the means and the urge to spend a few extra bucks on fun puppy stuff, also consider:

• Some dogs adore stuffed animals and carry them around everywhere like a security blanket. Others love gutting them and spreading the stuffing everywhere. You only need to try it once to find out which category your dog falls under. Some owners buy their destructive dogs stuffed animals even though they know it will make a mess, just to let their dogs have a little fun. Fleece-covered stuffed toys for dogs, often containing squeakers, are perennial favorites.

• Fill the Nylabone® Crazy Ball® with treats and when your dog rolls the ball, treats randomly dispense.

• Bows, jeweled collars, bandanas, and other high-fashion accessories.

• Gourmet pet treats. Some bakeries are totally devoted to pet treats, and many of them will ship their goodies. Check out Three Dog Bakery at www.threedog.com.

Some dogs love the luxury of a soft bed.

• While you're at it, why not go for the complete wardrobe? Thinly coated dogs require warmth in winter, but you can go the extra mile and make your dog the most fashionable pup on the block. Check out the Internet for great canine fashion, from T-shirts, visors, and sunglasses to fancy mock fur coats in jungle prints, 100-percent wool sweaters, leather motorcycle jackets, and even boots.

• Doggy cologne. Why shouldn't your dog smell as good as you do?

• Fancy dog furniture, usually designed for small dogs. Look for canopy beds, miniature couches, and lounge chairs. The ultimate luxury!

Puppy-Proofing Your Home

The last step before you bring your new puppy into your home is to puppy-proof the house. Puppies are curious, quick, able to squirm into spaces you wouldn't believe, and they can get into a lot of trouble…fast.

Interactive toys help to stimulate your puppy's mind.

Keep your pup safely confined when you can't supervise him.

Puppy Poison Control

What if your puppy licked up some tasty but highly toxic antifreeze from the garage? What if he got into some really rotten garbage? Did you know acetaminophen could kill your puppy and so could chocolate? Keep the National Animal Poison Control Center (NAPCC) number handy at all times: 888-426-4435. Their website also has lots of information about pet safety: http://www.aspca.org. If you call the NAPCC, you will be charged a $45 consulting fee to talk to a vet, but the fee is well worth a dog's life.

The problem is that you never know just what a puppy is going to do until she does it. Oops, there goes your new sock. Oops, apparently your puppy enjoys tug of war with the drapes. Oops, wasn't there a chicken on the table a few minutes ago, and where *is* that dog? The best way to make at least a fair guess about what your puppy might get into is to spend some time around your house at puppy level. Yes, that means down on the floor, about a foot off the ground. Look around—what do you see?

Think about what looks tempting to chew or play with. Remember that puppies explore with their mouths, so small objects—paper clips, stray buttons, little plastic toys—can be choking hazards, and garbage, plants, medications, and household chemicals can be poisonous. Keep the floor picked up and vacuumed.

Make sure your puppy has access to lots of chew toys so that whenever he zeroes in on something you don't want him to chew, you can quickly replace it with something he is allowed to chew. Soon he will learn to choose his own toys instead of your shoes.

Also make sure to keep garbage and houseplants inaccessible and keep medication, household cleaners, and other chemicals out of reach, including chemicals stored under sinks, in basements and garages, and in sheds. Automobile and lawn and garden products can be particularly hazardous outside, where we may not realize how accessible they are.

Once your home is neat, safe, and sound, make sure your puppy has a special spot for eating, a special spot for sleeping undisturbed, and lots of attention and supervision during those first months as he learns the house rules and you get to know each other better. Keep your puppy safe and the two of you may enjoy many happy years together.

Part 3

Great Health:
Year One and Beyond

The first few weeks with a new puppy in the house can seem to last for months. You've got a lot to teach your latest family member in order to help him learn how to live peacefully with the humans in the house. Puppies have a lot of behaviors people don't much like: they chew, they play-bite, they dig, they try to run away, and they think the world is their personal toilet.

In this chapter, we'll talk about some of the most important things you can do to keep your puppy healthy and happy in his youth. It's easy to think dogs don't need much when they are young. They seem so healthy and energetic. But puppies need health care maintenance, so they can stay strong and healthy. That includes making sure he gets his

Good health starts a puppy on the road to a happy life.

Dogs are social animals that need interaction with their owners.

A Hug a Day Keeps the Vet Away

When life gets busy, it's easy to forget about a dog, especially one who is well behaved. Don't let your relationship with your dog fall by the wayside. Build it by doing something to improve that relationship every single day. Never miss a day—let it be a habit, like brushing your teeth. Put it in your Palm Pilot or write it in your day planner in permanent marker. Whether that means ten minutes of daily cuddling with your puppy or a rousing game of fetch one day, a veg-out session in front of Animal Planet the next, do something—anything—to show your dog you remember she is there.

regular vaccinations, controlling pests, feeding your puppy a healthy diet, making sure he gets enough exercise, and building your relationship so your puppy has a healthy and satisfying emotional life as well as good physical health. It may sound like a lot to do for a little four-legged furry creature, but that's your job as a puppy companion.

Your Puppy/Human Relationship

Living with a dog is more than a matter of sharing your living space. Dogs are social animals and because they have been bred for centuries not only to live with but also to work and interact with humans, dogs are hardwired to need us. Sure, wild dogs can live without humans, but the domestic dogs we know and love won't be able to fulfill their potential without the partnership of people. No matter how smart your dog is, if you don't help to give her outlets to exercise her intelligence, you may never find out.

One of the best things about living with a dog is the dog-human relationship, but this relationship is also one of the easiest things to miss or ruin through bad management. Dog ownership entails getting to know this member of another species and becoming friends.

You've got many different ways to build a strong and healthy relationship with your dog. Training, playing, or simply spending time with your dog will all help your relationship. Miscommunications, anger, hitting, and ignoring your dog will quickly destroy that relationship.

Here are some ideas for building your puppy/human relationship, from early puppyhood well into your dog's adult years.

One-on-One Time

Don't let a day go by without spending some serious one-on-one time with your dog. In this case, quality counts for more than quantity. If you take just 15 minutes out of your day to pay attention to your dog and nothing else, you'll both feel closer and the bonding will go a long way toward making your dog feel like he is getting enough attention, which can allay all kinds of behavioral problems like nervous chewing, digging, and chronic barking. Dogs often misbehave because they aren't getting enough human interaction, so make sure you interact with your dog in a positive way.

Spend your bonding time petting, talking to, or playing with your dog. Turn off the TV if it distracts you from your buddy, and don't talk on the phone. Don't keep leaving to tend to the kids or other things, and don't make the time about rigorous training. Make it positive, fun, and preferably calm so your dog associates time with you with a feeling of tranquility rather than hyperactivity. Lots of quiet, relaxed stroking and "good dog's" are nice. Some gentle games can be fun, too. No tug-of-war, but perhaps some retrieving or running around together in the yard followed by some down time.

Spend quality time with your puppy every day.

Three 5-minute sessions at different times during the day work just as well as one 15-minute block.

On the Road

Every time you go somewhere in the car, whether a family vacation or a trip to the post office, take your dog with you, if possible. When you take your dog with you instead of leaving him at home, you get to spend more time together, plus he gets to experience different kinds of places and meet different people, which will help to make him better socialized.

Part 3

It is possible to take your dog with you when you travel.

Travel Savvy

Traveling with your dog can be great fun as long as you are prepared. Make sure you bring an adequate supply of food, a jug of the kind of water your dog normally gets (from your tap or purified), I.D. tags for your dog, a canine first aid kit, and a card with the telephone numbers of your vet and the animal poison control center. Also make sure the places you stay and visit allow dogs, or that you will have somewhere safe and secure for your dog to stay when you go somewhere that doesn't allow dogs. And remember to never, ever leave your dog alone in a parked car with closed windows, even when it is just a little bit warm outside.

One mistake some people make is bringing their puppies everywhere when they are small and manageable, but leaving them home once they are full grown. Your dog doesn't understand why you used to take him everywhere and now he must be left behind, and this will eventually erode your relationship. Do your job socializing and training your dog so his manners are so impeccable that you can take him anywhere you could take a puppy. Or, if you prefer puppy-sized portability, choose a smaller breed.

In either case, big dog or small, never miss an opportunity to bring your buddy with you when you hit the road.

Playtime

Puppies love to play, and older dogs enjoy it, too. If you are playful with your puppy instead of impatient, both of you will enjoy your time together much more. Throw a ball or a stick. Play gentle tug-of-war with small dogs (tug-of-war games can encourage larger dogs, especially guardian breeds, to be too aggressive). Chase your dog around the yard or practice tricks you've taught her. Go to the dog park or for a walk around the block or go exploring in a nearby natural area.

Tug-of-All-Out-War

If your dog loves tug-of-war but tends to get too rough, it is best to play a different game. Tug-of-war can encourage dogs to be dominant and even to act aggressively, especially if you play rough. Instead, teach your dog to chase a ball, fetch and retrieve, or catch a Frisbee™.

Dogs thrive when they are allowed to bond with their owners.

Life is full of interesting smells and sounds. Just about anything can become a toy or be made into a game. Tap into your dog's natural sense of play and the two of you will have a great time together. You'll both have a whole lot of fun and a stronger relationship, too.

Exercise

Puppies have a natural instinct to play. Playing with littermates teaches puppies about social interaction, and it also exercises those puppy muscles. When puppies are tiny, it's easy for them to get enough exercise, but when you bring a puppy home, you have to pick up where those littermates left off.

Exercise is just as important for dogs as it is for humans, and for all the same reasons. Exercise keeps excess weight off a dog. It keeps the heart in good working order. It keeps the joints limber and healthy. It also contributes to a

Exercise is important to your dog's physical and mental health.

Roly Poly Puppies

According to William Smith, DVM, veterinarian for the Iams Company in Dayton, Ohio, obesity is the most common nutritional disease among pets and one of the most common diseases across the board. Although there are no exact national statistics regarding pets and obesity, some vets estimate that between 24 to 40 percent of all dogs brought in to veterinary clinics are obese.

Basic training can help control your dog's excess energy.

positive, relaxed mental state. Regular exercise is one of the greatest gifts you can give your dog.

Obesity is incredibly common in pet dogs. Vets often express to me their concern that obesity is the most common problem among the pets they see in their offices. Except for rare cases that involve medical problems, dogs get obese for one reason: they eat too much and don't exercise enough.

A puppy's youth has four stages: early puppyhood (birth to six months), late puppyhood (six months to one year), adolescence (one to two or three years, depending on the breed), and young adulthood (two to three years to five to seven years, depending on the breed). Each of these stages has different exercise requirements and challenges you must help your puppy meet so he can enjoy a healthy, active life.

Exercise for Young Puppies: Damage Control

In early puppyhood, dogs naturally take care of their own exercise needs until they leave the whelping box. When you take your new puppy home, he will have a lot of energy: No, I mean a *lot* of energy. In fact, one of the biggest challenges of new puppies (beyond housetraining) is keeping up with all that energy, something many people find too challenging because they aren't prepared for it.

Puppies without outlets for their high-intensity energy often turn to destruction, and depending on your puppy's breed, that destruction can be pretty major. Consider the pair of female Bloodhound puppies that ate through their family's living room wall all the way to the dining room, right through the sheet rock, when they were left alone? Or what about the Afghan who ate the dashboard out of the car in which his human left him? Or the Golden Retriever/Sharpei mix who ate the molding from around the front door when his human companion went to work? New puppy owners lose shoes, clothing, underwear, even whole pieces of furniture–couches with juicy cushions; dining room chairs with nice, chewable legs; feather pillows too tempting not to gut and spread around the room with puppy abandon.

Young puppies need lots of playtime that stimulates them both physically and mentally. They need lots of activity with you to keep them busy. They need chew toys and they need to be taught what is and what is not acceptable for chewing. They also require leash training so they can eventually safely accompany you outside the perimeters of your fence.

If you set aside time every day, preferably at least twice a day in the morning and evening, to exercise your young puppy, you'll also be exercising damage control. A tired puppy is a well-behaved puppy, as dog trainers like to say.

Sound tiring to you? Look at it this way: You'll be getting some good exercise, too, so you'll both benefit. And if you really can't deal with puppy energy, adopt an adult dog instead.

Late Puppyhood:
Making Exercise a Part of Life

As your puppy enters the second half of her first year, she is continuing to grow quickly and is probably much larger than she was as a young puppy. This is a tough stage for puppies–they still feel like playful babies, but their bodies are big and gangly. They

Older and Wiser

Many people who have lived through their pet's puppyhood opt for an adult dog the second time around. Adult dogs that need new homes often integrate seamlessly into a household, especially if they have had good homes and were well trained before. You won't get to experience that adorable tiny puppy stage, but for many, avoiding housetraining, play biting, chewing, and puppy destruction is well worth the sacrifice.

Part 3

Discipline and training are the keys to a well-behaved dog.

Learning tricks keeps your dog mentally active.

still have the impulse to race around, leap onto comfy laps, and play, but they are much more apt to bump into things, knock things (and people) down, slide into walls, and generally wreak havoc.

Suddenly having to deal with the exercise needs of a 50-pound dog is a lot different than keeping a 5-pound puppy amused. Bigger bodies need vigorous exercise to stay in shape, and that puppy energy still needs just as much of an outlet as it did in the first six months—or even more.

By this stage, your puppy should be leash trained and you can take her on walks every day, something most dogs practically live for. That leash can be a signal to your puppy that something really, really great is about to happen. "You wanna go on a walk? You wanna go on a WALK?" Witness the leaps and twists and tail chasing such a request is sure to invoke in a dog that gets to go on regular walks.

Daily walks—some dogs thrive on two, and if you live in an apartment or house without a fenced yard, at least two walks are a requirement—establish an excellent habit for both you and your dog. Daily walks give you both exercise. They provide time together. They get you both out in the fresh air.

The Great Outdoors

More active types might really enjoy taking their dogs on runs, bike rides, or hikes in the wilderness. Dogs love to explore different surroundings. Just be sure to keep your dog safely on-leash in areas where she could get in trouble. Hazards to dogs are many in the wilderness—wild animals, rivers, cliffs, and barbed plants can all be dangerous to your pet. In most cases, leashes are crucial unless your dog really is reliably trained to stay by you and not run away. If your dog is a scenthound or sighthound breed, like a Beagle or a Greyhound, forget about off-leash exercise—keep the leash on at all times.

Part 3

Daily walks keep you both healthy–the brisker, the better, except in extreme temperatures–and they teach your dog the importance of good manners when out in the world.

In some cases, a daily walk isn't necessary. People who own toy dogs–especially those not able to go on walks–can get away with keeping their pets indoors. Very small dogs can get enough exercise playing fetch and gallivanting around the house. Any dog over 20 pounds, however, should really get some serious outdoor exercise.

If you absolutely can't find the time or the inclination to walk your dog, at least spend time every day outside engaging her in some vigorous play. If you teach her to retrieve, you can relax in your deck chair and throw the rope bone in perpetuity while she gets all the exercise, or enlist the kids to play chase or throw-the-tennis-ball for a good half-hour each day.

One last note about the daily walk: Dogs are creatures of habit. They love routines and while some dogs are more flexible than others, upsetting a dog's routine is sure to upset the dog. Daily walks are an excellent habit, but make sure you commit to the process. Sure, once in awhile you'll have to cancel a walk, but try to make it a regular occurance and not a sporadic when-I-feel-like-it kind of undertaking. Let your dog feel secure in the knowledge that every day, come 9 a.m., or 3 p.m., or 8:45 p.m., it's time for that walk. (Hey, routines are good for you, too. They help keep you organized.)

In the "teenage" years, your dog may regress in training.

Adolescents: Keeping Your Teen Dog Under Control

Just when you thought your puppy was starting to mellow; just when you thought the worst was over; just when you thought life was about to settle down into a calm, normal existence with a well behaved adult pet…boom, adolescence descends.

Dogs reach adolescence at about one year of age–some a little sooner, some a little later, depending on the breed. For some dogs, adolescence rears its ugly

Prey Drive

The prey drive, or the instinct to chase small animals, doesn't show up in some dogs until adolescence. Terriers and hounds are particularly likely to chase small animals, from squirrels on the lawn to escaped parakeets, but any breed has the potential for a strong prey drive. Please take precautions if you have small animals like cats, ferrets, rabbits, hamsters, or birds and keep them safe from your dog.

head for only a few months. For others, this trying "teen" time can last until your friend is two or three years of age.

Anyone who knows a human teenager knows that adolescence is stressful on the teens themselves, as well as on their families. Dogs are the same. Adolescent dogs are first experiencing the full force of sexual maturity if you haven't had them neutered. (Of course, you *have* had your pet neutered, right?) Even when they are neutered, adolescent dogs undergo some hormonal changes.

Adolescent dogs go through another big burst of energy akin to early puppyhood. Some adolescents are so overactive that their people find they can't handle them at all. Once again, energy unchanneled by you will probably be channeled by your dog into some kind of destruction, such as digging out and running away or other bad behavior, like excessive barking or sudden feistiness. That once-safe neighbor cat may suddenly be fair prey to your adolescent dog.

Adolescent dogs can be a real challenge behaviorally, too. They may become more defiant and less likely to do what you say. (Sound familiar, parents of teens?) They may get particularly interested in other dogs or particularly dog-aggressive. They may try to dash off when you least expect it, or they may become totally immersed in whatever interesting activity you decide to teach them, like agility, flyball, Frisbee™, or long-distance running.

Adolescent dogs, especially males (but this can happen to females, too), may become more aggressive, testing you to see if you really are the more dominant one. Training and proper management can quickly bring these tendencies under control, because no dog should ever be allowed to behave aggressively toward humans.

Managing Aggression

If your adolescent dog begins to show signs of aggression based in delusions of dominance-grandeur, you have to act and act fast. Signs that your dog is testing you or other members of your family, include:

• Growling when you approach him while he is eating.

• Pushing against you to try to move you or control your direction while walking.

• "Leading" you around the house by going first to the back door, to the kitchen, or wherever he knows you are headed.

• Growling if you try to move him off the bed or couch (he is taking possession).

• Growling to protect toys or other possessions.

• Showing more aggressive behavior toward other dogs, children, or other pets.

How do you handle emerging dominant behavior? For anyone remotely uncomfortable with their pets, hiring a professional is an absolute necessity. Look for canine behavioral consultants, animal behaviorists, or trainers who specialize in dog aggression, have good references, and whose methods are non-violent and humane. An aggressive dog, especially a large one, can

Training and proper management can help bring aggressive tendencies under control.

Part 3

Your Canine Liability

Dog aggression is a big issue these days. Mismanaged large dogs that are allowed to become too aggressive have injured and even killed people, and the owners of those dogs are subject to huge liabilities. Dog bites are all too common—4.7 million annually in the US, some 800,000 serious enough to cause hospitalization. Sixty percent of dog bite victims are children, and every year in the US, a few people die from dog attacks. Dog aggression has led to legislation, sometimes misdirected, that seeks to ban certain breeds. Insurance companies can deny coverage to pet owners with certain breeds of dog. Landlords can refuse to lease to dog owners, and some cities have banned certain breeds of dog, most typically pit bull breeds, Rottweilers, and Doberman Pinschers. Managing your dog so that he never becomes aggressive is the best way to avoid personal trouble and send the message to society in general that well managed dogs can be very good dogs, no matter what their breed.

If your dog displays dominant tendencies, you may want to enlist professional help.

be very dangerous, and sometimes that aggression comes from a health problem or has a genetic basis that is not your fault.

In other cases, dogs with very dominant personalities are simply mismanaged by owners who either should have chosen a less-dominant breed or individual because they aren't themselves particularly dominant or who mishandle or mistreat a dog. If you adopted a dog who had a previous owner, that owner may have mistreated the dog or failed to socialize and train him.

Some people are in a situation where they are willing to take the risk to rehabilitate an aggressive dog. Some people, such as those with small children or neighbors with small children, may not want to take that risk and should seek help or contact a rescue group for advice. However, if your adolescent Rottie, Dobie, or German Shepherd is simply testing you to make sure you are still in charge, there are certainly things you can do to send him a clear message that yes, you are in charge, thank you very much!

Your dominant dog must be reminded on a daily basis who is in charge. This does *not* mean you should behave aggressively toward your dog. Playing his game won't work because he will win. He's the dog, and he's the expert. The trick is to play *your* game and make him follow your rules because you are the expert at being the human. You can walk on two legs, for goodness sake! You can do math! You can speak! You're the boss!

Winning at the dominance game does mean behaving assertively and with impeccable consistency. Especially in the case of large dogs, I cannot overemphasize the importance of asserting yourself as the leader. Theories vary about how much of a pack mentality dogs really have, whether they really do think in terms of an "alpha" and so forth. Whether or not they do, dogs need someone to be in charge of them, just like children do. They aren't versed in the behavior acceptable to human society and since you are, you have to be the responsible one.

You: The Best Dog on the Block

As a trainer once told me (I'm paraphrasing), the only way to be in charge is to be the most clever, most unusual, most amazing "dog" in the house, the one who your dog can only aspire to resemble. If they want to be just like you, you will win. If you try to be like them, forget about it. They will run the show.

Because you can't outrun, or in the case of large dogs, manhandle your canine friend, you have to have the mental edge, and you have to be the leader. If your dog is secure in the fact that someone else sets the rules and enforces them benevolently, he will be happy to follow your lead. He'll even be relieved.

Some tricks for managing dominant dogs I've collected over the years include:

• No free lunches! This is a policy I recommend for any dog owner, which is to never give your dog anything he really likes without making him work for it first. Make him sit, lie down, or do a trick before you give him any treat, ever. Make him sit or lie down as you fill his food bowl and after you set it on the floor, make him stay for a few seconds before he is allowed to eat. Release him with an "OK" command.

• Don't let your dog lead you around the house if he is tending toward dominant behavior. Every time my dog wants to go out, she gets my attention but then waits as I walk past her and obediently follows me to the back door. If your dog tries to insist on leading you around, be even more insistent. Stop, tell your dog to sit, walk ahead of him, then release him. If he darts ahead of you again, stop, and repeat the process. He'll soon get the idea.

• Put a moratorium on letting your dog sleep on your bed, or even sit on the sofa. If he has forgotten who is in charge, it is your job to remind him. So he looks at you with pleading eyes at bedtime? Put his dog

Let your dog work for his treats and praise by performing basic obedience.

Part 3

Are You Spoiling Your Dog?

Don't feel guilty about letting your dog sleep on your bed or curl up on the couch with you if he doesn't have dominance issues. This is a tactic to help dogs understand who's in charge. Some dogs already know you are on top of the totem pole and will be perfectly well behaved, couch time and all.

The household rules should be consistently reinforced.

bed or kennel in your room but make him lie down there or on the floor, not on the bed with you. If he begs to jump up on the couch, command him to lie down on the floor while you watch TV. He'll soon get the picture. Eventually, after he matures, you can occasionally reward him with a night on the bed or a snuggle on the couch for good behavior.

• Humans find eye contact natural, but dogs, behaviorist theorize, see eye contact as a challenge. While you may think it is best to challenge your dog and win, a more successful strategy is to refuse to engage in a challenge. You are way too smart a dog for that! Very dominant dogs will get the message that you are more dominant if you refuse to make eye contact for a few days. You can talk to them, feed them, play with them, walk them, even pet them, but don't make eye contact. Act uninterested. They will soon be rolling over like a submissive puppy to get your attention. When you do make eye contact, do it briefly.

• Some experts also recommend a temporary stay on petting and affection, which your dog may interpret as a sign of you giving in to his desires. Try singing and talking to him and taking him on walks, but forego the mushy, lovey behavior for awhile. He'll get the message.

• Exercise, exercise, exercise! Some people theorize that aggression can stem from the frustration that comes from not getting enough physical and mental exercise. Large dogs in particular may find it difficult to get enough exercise to release all their energy because you can't run fast enough for them and those short little walks around the block just aren't doing the trick. Large breeds need lots of room to run and romp. If you don't have a fenced yard, find a place to take your dog on a regular basis where he can run freely in an enclosed area free

Dogs Allowed

One important caution: If you choose to let your dog loose in a public place, be sure that the location allows dogs! Breaking rules makes dog owners everywhere look bad and may contribute to more anti-dog laws and regulations.

from the dangers of traffic or other distractions, such as a dog park, a friend's yard, a deserted sports field or school grounds, or anywhere else where he can be free of a leash but can't run away. If you have no such place, at least increase your daily walks and backyard playtime, significantly if possible, or hire a pet sitter to come and walk or play with your dog in the middle of the day. The point is to wear that puppy out! Again, a tired dog is a good dog, and a large dog that is well exercised on a daily basis may be less likely to exercise dominant behavior.

Once your dog's dominant behavior is under control, you can gradually shift the house rules to be more amendable to both of you, but just as with kids, consistency and assertive authority are crucial to good behavior. That never means violence or being nasty to your dog. It simply means enforcing the sensible rules that are in everyone's best interest. Your dog will love you for it, and you'll be much less likely to give up on your dominant friend.

If you find these tips don't work, or if you feel intimidated by or unable to handle your pet's aggression, again, I strongly suggest hiring a professional canine behavioral consultant or trainer who specializes in aggression. In this day and age, nobody can afford to live with a dangerous dog. Then again, not every dog that growls or nips is dangerous. You have to be experienced enough to know the difference, and if you aren't, a professional can help you.

In some rare and unfortunate cases, extreme aggression is too much of a liability and not practically or easily cured. Vets and behavioral consultants alike may recommend putting such a dog to sleep. Much preferable, of course, is to avoid allowing a dog to get to this point.

A well-exercised dog is a happy, tired dog that will stay out of trouble.

Part 3

Is He or Isn't He?

Growling isn't always a sign of aggression. Sometimes it is a message that your dog has had enough. People shouldn't bother your dog when she is eating, drinking, or resting in her bed or kennel. Teach your children, especially, not to poke and prod your dog, pull her skin, ears, or tail, or otherwise tease her. Dogs and children should always be supervised. When your dog has reached the limits of her patience, she may growl, and only you can judge whether your dog is being aggressive or has just reached the end of her rope after too much harassment.

Young Adults:
Exercise Now for a Lifetime of Good Health

Ahhhhhh. At last, your pet is settling down. She's not quite as hyper as she was in her adolescence. Her energy level has dropped off, she isn't so prone to chewing, she is fully housetrained, she knows the rules, she enjoys playing and training and hanging out with you, and everyone is getting along beautifully. Isn't it nice when those teenagers finally hit their twenties?

But young adults need exercise, too, even as they settle down. Keeping up good exercise habits in your dog's young adulthood could help her avoid many of the diseases of aging she could encounter later, like obesity, heart problems, arthritis, and even cancer. Your dog should get some vigorous exercise every day to keep her acting and feeling young. Spending time walking and playing together will also continue to strengthen and solidify your relationship.

And don't forget how good those daily walks are for you, too! If you stay healthy, you can be a better family member, and that benefits everyone, including your dog.

In Sickness and In Health

We all hope our dogs will live long, happy lives, but sometimes dogs get sick and as their caretakers, we must know what to do for them to keep them as healthy as possible and to help them recover as quickly as possible. Because dogs have shorter life spans than humans, most dog lovers have lost a friend or two, but solid knowledge, frequent veterinary checkups, vigilance, and sound practice of prevention should help your dog live out a normal lifespan. This chapter will start you on that path.

Of course, you are already headed down the right path if you have taken your new puppy to a veterinarian for a checkup, if you are making sure your puppy is getting all those important first-year

Preventive health care is essential to the well-being of your dog.

Daily petting and grooming will help you monitor your dog's health.

vaccinations, if you feed him a well-balanced diet, and if you are doing your weekly grooming exam. But knowing what to look for–what a healthy dog looks and acts like, and what could indicate a health problem–could save your dog's life.

The Healthy Dog

What does a healthy pet dog look like? You probably already know. A healthy dog has a shiny coat, bright eyes, a moist nose, sharp white teeth, smooth and supple skin, flexible paw pads, short nails. A healthy dog feels good, is free from pain, can move easily and freely, has enough energy to play and exercise, eats well, sleeps well, and enjoys human company.

What can you do to keep your healthy dog as healthy as she can be for as long as possible? Several very important things:

√ Pay attention. The weekly grooming exam and time spent with your dog each day will help you to monitor your dog's health.

√ Schedule an annual exam. Your vet is trained to detect problems you may not notice and will also do standard tests to make sure your dog is healthy.

√ Keep up on first-year vaccinations to prevent infectious diseases.

√ Supervise your dog and don't let him roam loose where he could pick up diseases and/or become injured.

Signs Something Could be Wrong

If you pay attention to your dog's behavior, eating and drinking habits, skin, coat, eyes, ears, nose, mouth, and paws, you will notice when something changes. A change in habits or in your dog's body should always put you on the alert. However, you can keep an eye out for some specific things that could signal a health problem. Each section in this chapter will have an alert list, but some of the general signs of a health problem include the following and are worth a call to the vet:

• Sudden noticeable increase or decrease in appetite, especially lasting more than a day or two

• Sudden noticeable increase in thirst (drinking water more often)

• Any lumps, bumps, itching, or irritated skin patches

• Hair loss

• Ear shaking or scratching

• Red, swollen, or runny eyes

• Discharge from nose

• Red, irritated, or receding gums

• Noticeable plaque on teeth

• Cracked paw pads

• Limping or favoring a leg

• Yelping in pain when touched

• Sudden inability to jump up or down from couches, beds, etc.

• Sudden reluctance to climb stairs

• Sudden refusal to be active, run, or jump

• Suddenly moving more slowly

• Uncharacteristic irritability or lethargy

• Sleeping more than normal, especially lasting more than a day or two

• Doesn't seem to hear

• Doesn't seem to see well, bumps into things

• Disorientation

• Acts uncharacteristically nervous, jumpy, or depressed

• Displays uncharacteristically low energy

Again, any of these symptoms could have simple explanations and easy solutions, but they could also indicate more serious health problems, so please don't ignore changes in your pet.Stay in contact with your vet, your best ally in the quest to keep your dog healthy and happy.

Give a Dog a Pill

If you find your dog does have a health condition, you may need to give her medication that is prescribed by or recommended by your vet, and chances are, that medication will be in pill form.

Some dogs are happy to swallow a pill buried in a bit of cheese, meat paste (like liverwurst), canned dog food, or peanut butter. Others will find that pill, no matter how small, and spit it right back out. Always watch your dog if you give him a pill with food to be absolutely sure he swallows it. If he won't, you'll have to make sure the pill gets down that throat. Here's how.

1. Call your dog to you and hold his collar gently. Reassure him and calm him with gentle words and petting. If your dog is nervous or resistant, you may need another pair of hands to help hold and calm him (some dogs don't mind).

2. With one hand, place your thumb right behind one of your dog's canine teeth (the long sharp ones on the top to the side), which will cause your dog to open his mouth.

3. Holding the pill or capsule with your other hand, use that hand to push your dog's lower jaw down. Place the pill as far back as you can on the middle of your dog's tongue. If you put it to the side, your dog can spit it out easily.

4. Close your dog's mouth and massage his throat until he swallows.

5. When your dog licks his nose, you will know he has swallowed the pill.

Liquids, Injections, and Suppositories

If your dog's medication isn't in pill form, it will be in the form of a liquid to be swallowed or injected or in suppository form. Your vet can show you how to administer all these forms of medication, but liquids and suppositories are usually easy to give your dog.

To administer liquid medicine from a syringe, hold your dog's head around the ears, pull back the side of his mouth, insert the syringe (or eyedropper) into the cheek pouch, hold his lips around the syringe so medicine can't leak out, tilt your dog's head back, and dispense the medicine. Your dog should swallow automatically.

Your dog may need a suppository if he is unable to keep pills or liquid in his stomach due to vomiting. A suppository must be lubricated with petroleum jelly and inserted into the anal canal.

To give your dog an injection, such as in the case of a severe allergic reaction or if your pet is diabetic and requires insulin, have your vet demonstrate the correct method. Injections are either subcutaneous, which means they are administered just under the skin and typically are not painful, or intramuscularly, which means they must be injected directly into the muscle. Your dog may find these momentarily painful and you may need someone to help you hold your dog.

How to Take a Dog's Temperature

A dog's normal temperature averages 101.3 degrees Fahrenheit but can range from 100 degrees to 102.5 degrees. A newborn puppy's temperature is

You may need to give medication to your dog.

You should know how to take your dog's temperature.

Part 3

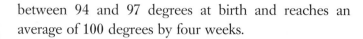

between 94 and 97 degrees at birth and reaches an average of 100 degrees by four weeks.

If you suspect your dog is sick and your vet wants to know, over the phone, if she has a temperature, you must know how to take her temperature. Obviously, your dog isn't going to hold a thermometer in her mouth, so you must take a rectal temperature. Use a bulb thermometer or, for faster and easier reading, a digital thermometer available at any drugstore.

Rub the bulb with a little petroleum jelly. Hold up your dog's tail, which will keep her in a standing position, and insert the thermometer with a twisting motion one to three inches into the anal canal (farther in for larger dogs). Hold the thermometer in place for three minutes or, in the case of a digital thermometer, until it beeps indicating it is finished. Read the thermometer, then clean it with alcohol.

R&R for Dogs

Some conditions require enforced rest, such as spinal disc ruptures. Sometimes called crate rest, this treatment depends on your dog keeping still so he can heal, sometimes for days at a time. This is a common treatment for Dachshunds and other long-backed dogs with canine intervertebral disc disease. Your dog must be confined to his crate except for bathroom breaks and encouraged to stay still and rest.

While a sick dog probably won't want to move around much, once pain medications kick in and your dog starts to feel better, he will probably be itching to get out and play. He may whine, cry, beg, plead, and gaze at you with such a pathetic expression that you may be tempted to give in and let him out for just a little while.

Thermometer Mishaps

Occasionally a dog will sit while having his temperature taken, and this could cause a glass thermometer to break off. If this happens, do not try to remove the thermometer. Call your vet or emergency pet care clinic immediately for instructions. Avoid this possibility by using a plastic digital thermometer.

Some health conditions may require your dog to limit his activity.

Part 3

Do Dogs Suffer from Stress?

Dogs—like any animal—can suffer from stress. Dogs are creatures of habit with a strong survival instinct and become agitated when their routines are broken or when they think they are in danger. This natural survival mechanism results in certain physiological changes: increased heart, blood pressure and respiratory rates; adrenaline surges; blood pumping to muscles and away from the digestive system. Too much agitation over a long period can result in chronic stress. Your dog's body isn't designed to undergo the physiological stress state very often, as this is meant for emergencies. Maybe your routine has changed. You moved to a new home, got a new job, had a baby, adopted a cat. Or, maybe you've found a stray that has been living a stressful or possibly abusive existence. Patience, understanding, and a calming environment with good health care, sound nutrition, exercise, and plenty of love should eventually bring your stressed-out pet back to normal. Talk to your vet if your pet seems to be suffering from extreme anxiety or depression, or if you have found a stray dog that is very agitated, shy, aggressive, or fearful. Such behavior could also be the result of a physical problem. Anxious behavior can result in physical problems, and physical problems can result in anxious behavior, but rather than play "which came first," have your pet treated by a professional.

Please follow your doctor's orders when it comes to crate rest. It could mean the difference between a future of normal function and a future of rear-leg paralysis for your dog. Remember who's the boss and don't let that wily puppy convince you otherwise.

Prevention

Certainly the most effective method of health care is prevention. The better care you take of your dog, the less likely he will be to get sick. Of course, you can't do anything about genetic disease, and sometimes pets get sick for reasons we can't trace. However, a consistent schedule, good food, moderate exercise, lots of bonding time with you, and regular vet visits will go a long way to ensure your pet stays as healthy as possible.

But you can do more, especially when it comes to preventing pests like fleas, ticks, and heartworms, that not only make your dog uncomfortable but very ill. You can also do certain things to keep your dog's skin and coat in great shape, and to prevent your dog from contracting infectious diseases.

Part 3

If your dog is scratching excessively, he may have fleas.

Part 3

Pest Control

Most pet owners have had at least some experience with fleas. People who take their pets into wooded areas have probably also seen a tick or two. Pests like heartworms borne through the bite of a mosquito, tapeworms borne through the bite of a flea, and various kinds of mites may go unnoticed until serious symptoms emerge, making prevention crucial.

Probably the most common pest that pet owners must contend with are fleas, so let's look first at how to control fleas and all the problems they can cause for you and your pet.

Flea-Free

Fleas are ubiquitous. Almost any dog that spends time outside in warm weather, especially around other dogs, will probably get a flea bite or two. In many cases, because fleas are opportunistic feeders and breeders, a few fleas will quickly become an infestation. You can tell if your pet has fleas by using a flea comb or your fingers to examine his skin, especially around the ears, underside, and groin area. Fleas are tiny brown insects, about two millimeters long. They crawl or jump and are difficult to catch, even more difficult to crush between your fingers. If you remove them mechanically from your pet with a flea comb, drop them in rubbing alcohol to kill them, then flush them down the toilet.

Even if you don't see fleas, you may see flea dirt (little brownish-red specks of digested blood) and flea eggs (little white specks). Both are indicators that fleas are crawling around somewhere.

Fleas bite your dog to feed on blood. In a pinch, they may even bite you. Flea bites itch, and some dogs that are allergic to flea saliva can develop a condition called flea bite dermatitis, which causes severe itching and red, raw spots. Fleas can also transit tapeworms to your dog.

The most common flea to bite pet dogs is actually called the cat flea, or *C. felis*. At any time, only about one percent of the fleas in an environment (like your home) will be on your dog in adult form. The rest will be in egg, larval, or pupal form in carpets, furniture, and grass. That means getting rid of fleas is usually a multi-step process.

Fortunately, science has provided pet owners with an alternative to the messy and often toxic sprays, dips, foggers, and collars once required for flea control. Topical spot-on products, which are available through your veterinarian, should be applied monthly during flea season (in some areas such as the South and Southwest, flea season can be all year long).

Be sure to check your dog's coat for parasites after playing outdoors.

Spot-ons are liquids contained in one-application tubes, applied to the skin between your dog's shoulder blades and, in the case of large dogs, at the base of the tail. Follow product directions carefully. The product moves along the skin and kills adult fleas on contact within 12-24 hours and is nontoxic because it doesn't enter your dog's bloodstream. For mild infestations, spot-ons may be enough when used monthly because, as the remaining flea eggs hatch and the larvae develop and eventually become adult fleas, they will be killed when they jump on your dog.

Caution for Cats

Some chemicals used in flea products for dogs are very toxic to cats. Never use a flea control product designed for dogs on a cat. Dog and cat flea control products are not interchangeable! Always follow package directions for any flea control product to prevent toxicity for your pet and for you.

Severe infestations may require a more complete approach: a flea dip or bath with flea shampoo, application of a spot-on, and a spray for carpets, furniture, and yard containing an adulticide to kill adult fleas as well as an insect growth regulator (IGR) to keep flea eggs from hatching. Vigilance all summer long, including frequent laundering of bedding and vacuuming of carpets and soft furniture, should keep fleas under control.

Part 3

Other Pests and How to Treat Them

PEST	SYMPTOMS	DANGERS
Scabies Mites (sarcoptic mange)	Severe itching, rash, hair loss, crusty ear tips	Very contagious, extreme scratching can damage skin, can transmit to humans
Cheyletiella mange mites (walking dandruff): most common in puppies from pet shops and kennels	Red bumpy rash, large flakes of dandruff in young puppies	Very contagious, can transmit to humans
Flies and maggots: injured or ill strays or severely neglected dogs are most at risk.	Maggots infest and infect open wounds and mats in coat on old, sick, or weak dogs.	Severe bacterial infection can cause shock and even death
Heartworms: Most at risk are dogs that spend more time outdoors and those living in southeastern Atlantic and Gulf Coast regions	Can cause fatigue, cough, weight loss, rapid breathing, fainting, bulging chest, and death	Loss of health and eventually, death
Intestinal worms (such as hookworms, roundworms, threadworms, whipworms, tapeworms, ascarids): many dogs have them and their systems keep them in check, but immune-suppressed and stressed dogs may develop an infection	Diarrhea, anemia, weight loss, blood in feces	Some intestinal worms can also infect humans and can cause serious diseases; children often affected by eating dirt or sand in feces-soiled environment
Protozoan diseases: such as giardiasis, trichomoniasis, and coccidiosis	Diarrhea, sometimes bloody	Giardiasis could be transmitted to humans, probably through infected water supply
Demodectic mange mite: occurs mainly in puppies and debilitated dogs	Patchy hair loss, scales, draining and crusty sores	Can result in skin infections and skin may permanently compromise skin and haircoat; may be genetic so affected dogs shouldn't be bred
Ringworm: not actually a parasite, though often mistaken for one, ringworm is a fungus that affects hair follicles	Hair loss in a circular pattern surrounded by a red ring and containing a scaly center	Can result in a bacterial skin infection; often transmitted to humans, frequently to children, through contact
Ear mites	Itching and scratching of ears, violent head shaking	Highly contagious, though not to humans; can cause bacterial infections

Part 3

PREVENTION	TREATMENT
Avoid contact with infected animals	Requires treatment by a vet, to include shampooing and subsequent periodic dipping with appropriate chemicals, spraying environment with appropriate chemicals, and treating dog with corticosteroids for itching and antibiotics for infected skin.
Avoid contact with infected animals, often found in pet shops and kennel	Shampoo with pyrethrin shampoo, dip with 2% lime-sulfur dip, following package instructions, treat all exposed animals
Keep dog well groomed and well cared for. Treat and keep clean all wounds/sores. Have strays with this condition treated by a vet to address larger health picture.	Remove maggots with tweezers and wash wound with Betadine solution, followed with pyrethrin spray. Infections require veterinary treatment and oral antibiotics.
Yearly heartworm test and monthly heartworm preventive medication from one month prior to mosquito season to one month after first frost, all year in warm climates, as directed by your veterinarian.	In mild cases, treatment with a drug to kill worms; in severe cases, surgical removal of worms. Heartworm tests are required before administering heartworm preventive.
De-worming puppy as directed by veterinarian, then keeping your dog in a clean, dry environment, off dirt surface. Keep lawns mowed and pick up stools in environment (kennel and yard); feed healthy diet to boost immunity.	Heartworm preventive controls some intestinal worms;
Avoid drinking from streams and lakes	Most treated with antiprotozoan medication like Flagyl
Keep immune system strong with good health habits; some breeds may be genetically susceptible	Must be treated by a veterinarian with medicated shampoos and dips for several months; skin infections treated with antibiotics, healthy diet to boost immunity
Avoid contact with infected dogs	Have a veterinarian diagnose ringworm. Treated with topical antifungal cream, bacterial infections treated with antibiotics.
Keep ear canals clean and dry	Treat all pets in the household; clean ears thoroughly and medicate to kill mites, as advised by your vet.

Part 3

Regular grooming is the best way to control parasites like fleas and ticks.

Ticked Off

Ticks are also common in most areas of the US, although the variety of tick differs according to geographical location. Ticks can cause serious diseases in your dog (and in you) such as Lyme disease and Rocky Mountain Spotted Fever. Ticks can attach to your dog anywhere, but are common around the ears, feet, and belly. After your dog has spent time in any wooded area (even a residential yard with large trees), examine her (and yourself) for ticks.

Ticks feed on blood by inserting their heads under the skin. As they drink, their bodies swell and once they are engorged, they drop off. If you find a tick crawling on your dog, immediately remove it with a tweezers and drop it in rubbing alcohol to kill it, then flush it down the toilet. If a tick is attached, soak a cotton ball with rubbing alcohol, nail polish remover, or a product designed to kill ticks (ask your pet store retailer) and apply it to the tick until it removes its head.

Never try to burn or smother a tick, and never touch a tick with your bare fingers. If an engorged tick bursts, the bacteria in its system could be hazardous to you. Always wear rubber gloves when handing ticks. Remove ticks with a tweezers or with special tick-removing tools available at pet stores or on the Internet.

Keep a Healthy Coat

The pests listed in the previous chart and their secondary conditions such as skin infections and allergic reactions are a major cause of skin and coat problems in dogs, but dogs can suffer from other skin and coat disorders, too. Canine skin is thinner than human skin, and if it is damaged, it can quickly become susceptible to infection.

The best way to keep your dog's skin and coat healthy is to keep your dog well groomed with frequent brushing and not-too-frequent shampooing, so the skin's natural oils can keep skin supple and coat shiny and resilient. Also, your dog should be on a high-quality food that doesn't cause an allergic reaction (your vet can test for food allergies) and which contains enough essential fatty acids to keep skin in good condition. Keeping your dog's coat free of tangles and mats is also essential, since a matted coat can attract dirt and parasites, contributing to skin problems.

Catching any skin or coat changes early can help your vet diagnose and treat skin problems and diseases, of which there are many. Skin diseases come in different forms: some result in severe itching, like flea-bite dermatitis, flea-allergy dermatitis, and other skin conditions caused by pests; some are food allergy dermatitis; and some are skin irritation due to contact with an irritant. Hormone disorders and genetic disorders can cause hair loss. Some conditions become infections with swelling, redness, and discharge. Other conditions are the result of immune-related or autoimmune-related conditions, and some are related to tumors, cysts, nodules, ulcers, and abscesses.

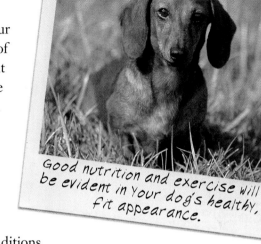

Good nutrition and exercise will be evident in your dog's healthy, fit appearance.

Alert your vet if you notice any of the following skin conditions on your dog:

- Itching

- Rashes

- Lumps

- Spots

- Skin flakes

- Hair loss

- Skin discoloration

- Swelling (general or localized)

- Crusts and scales

- Drainage

- Swollen hair follicles

- Odor

- Inflammation and redness within skinfolds

- Nodules, growths

- Ulcers, non-healing wounds

Infectious Diseases

Infectious diseases are different than inherited diseases because your dog "catches" them in some way, rather than being born with them. The best way to prevent infectious diseases is through regular vaccinations in the first year and subsequent vaccinations as recommended by your vet for your individual pet. While scientists haven't developed canine vaccines for all infectious diseases, those most serious and most common in dogs should be covered by your dog's regular vaccination protocol.

Distemper Risk

The canine distemper virus is the leading cause of death in dogs worldwide, although not in the US, where distemper vaccines are routine. All unvaccinated dogs are at high risk for distemper. Distemper is most dangerous to weak, malnourished, or immune-suppressed dogs. It attacks brain cells, skin, eyes, mucous membranes, and the gastrointestinal tract. Symptoms are a high fever of 103 to 105 degrees Fahrenheit, loss of appetite, lethargy, and discharge from eyes and nose, followed by coughing, abdominal blisters, vomiting, and diarrhea. Dogs then seem to recover, but are then struck down again with neurological symptoms like attacks of head shaking, strange jaw movements, jerking, and seizures. Even in dogs that recover, some neurological symptoms may persist. One rare form of distemper causes hard calluses to form on paw pads. Distemper must be treated by a veterinarian. Treatment consists solely of supportive therapies like antibiotics for secondary bacterial infections, intravenous fluids for dehydration, and medications (such as anticonvulsants) to relieve symptoms. A dog's own immune system must handle the virus itself, but the best treatment is prevention through vaccination, which is almost 100-percent effective against the disease.

Part 3

Infectious diseases come in several types:

1. **Bacterial diseases** are spread by contact with bacteria, typically from urine, feces, or other bodily secretions of an infected animal. In the case of Lyme disease, the bacteria are spread through a tick bite. Other examples of bacterial diseases include leptospirosis, brucellosis, bordatella, e. coli, and salmonella.

2. **Viral diseases** are spread through contact with the bodily secretions of an infected dog, including the inhalation of airborne viruses like the canine distemper virus, bites from an infected animal such as from a bat, skunk, fox, coyote, raccoon, or of course another dog with rabies, or through other contact with infected urine, feces, or saliva. Other examples of viral diseases include infectious canine hepatitis, canine herpes virus, canine coronavirus, and canine parvovirus.

3. **Fungal diseases** can infect the skin and mucus membranes (as with ringworm or yeast infections) or can infect a dog internally. Fungal diseases are contracted through contact with fungus spores that can enter the body through a wound in the skin or through inhalation. Fungal diseases are more common in malnourished or chronically ill dogs. They are typically characterized by diarrhea, vomiting, weight loss, and fever, and systemic forms can involve the lungs, liver, lymph nodes, brain, and spleen and can include severe neurological symptoms. Anti-fungal drugs are the typical treatment. Examples of fungal diseases include coccidioidomycosis, histoplasmosis, cryptococcosis, and blastomycosis.

Dogs can pick up diseases from other dogs, so keep up-to-date on vaccinations.

Make sure your dog has fresh food and water at all times.

Part 3

4. **Protozoan diseases** are caused by protozoa, one-celled parasites that invade the body, typically through the ingestion of raw or undercooked meat, through contact with feces or drinking water containing the protozoa, or through feces from infected insects contaminating an insect bite. Common symptoms are severe diarrhea, lethargy, pain, discharge from the eyes and nose, and severe weight loss, depending on the protozoa. Treatment consists of an appropriate medication to kill the protozoa, such as Flagyl or certain antibiotics. Examples of protozoan disease include toxoplasmosis (more common in cats), coccidiosis, trichomoniasis, and giardiasis.

5. **Rickettsial diseases** are caused by bacteria-sized parasites that invade cells and are usually transmitted through insects such as ticks. Examples of rickettsial diseases are canine ehrlichiosis and Rocky Mountain Spotted Fever.

Infectious diseases often (but not always) come on suddenly and severely. They should always be diagnosed and treated by your veterinarian.

System Disorders

Many other canine diseases affect different systems of your dog's body. While your vet should always be the one to diagnose your dog, below are some of the diseases and disorders that can afflict different anatomical systems in your dog. Knowing what to look for can help you to help your vet.

Hot Spot!

Hot spots are moist, pus-filled, painful patches of skin caused by a vicious cycle of itching and scratching due to allergies, dermatitis, or other skin irritations. Hot spots hurt! They are common in long-coated dogs because they can begin under mats or where skin irritation is less likely to be detected early, but hot spots can happen on any dog. Once they start, hot spots grow quickly and can be hard to resolve because dogs tend to continue to aggravate hot spots once they start. Talk to your vet about the best way to treat a hot spot, which may involve anesthetic, shaving the area, and treating with a special shampoo and an antibiotic steroid cream for several weeks, along with oral antibiotics and oral corticosteroids. Your vet may also recommend an Elizabethan collar to keep your dog from aggravating the area further.

Part 3

Skin and Coat Problems

We've already talked about all the ways in which parasites can compromise your dog's skin and coat, but skin and coat problems exist beyond the parasitic and fungal. Your dog's skin and coat may show the very first symptoms of a health problem, so pay close attention to them, both in grooming and in your everyday interactions with your dog. Signs your dog may have a health problem related to skin and coat include:

- Hives

- Rashes

- Lumps

- Cysts

- Bumps

Disorders of the skin and coat are common in dogs. Some dogs have allergies not only to flea bites but also to foods they eat, necessitating special diets, or things they contact in their environment, from shampoos to flea collars to plants.

Allergies can manifest as hives, rashes, itchy bumps, hair loss, and hot spots. Skin can also be injured through accidents, repeated contact against a surface, or from obsessive licking. Sometimes skin conditions indicate other problems. A thyroid deficiency can cause hair loss, and so can other hormonal imbalances such as too much cortisone or too much estrogen–or even too little estrogen. Hair loss can also be caused by a number of hereditary skin diseases, but keeping your dog's coat well brushed and skin checked carefully every week will allow you to spot skin and coat problems easily.

Disorders of the skin and coat are common in dogs.

Part 3

Check your dog's eyes for any problems on a daily basis.

Eyes/Ears/Nose/Throat

Your dog's eyes, ears, nose, and throat are largely visible to you, so if you pay attention during your weekly grooming exam, you may be more likely to notice when something goes wrong in these areas.

Signs that your dog is having a problem with his eyes, ears, nose, or throat include:

• Discharge from the eyes, nose, or ears

• Redness, irritation, or swelling

• Choking, coughing, gagging

• Nodules or other lumps along the eyelids or nose

• Ear scratching and shaking

• Constant sneezing

• Mouth breathing

• Bleeding from eyes, ears, nose, or mouth

Some of the more common disorders of the eyes, ears, nose, and throat include cataracts, glaucoma, progressive retinal atrophy (a degenerative eye disease leading to blindness), eyeball dislocation (most common in dogs with protruding eyes like Boston Terriers, Pugs, and Pekingese), entropion (turned-in eyelids), ectropion (rolled-out eyelid), eyelid tumors, cherry eye (a prolapsed tear gland on the third eyelid), conjunctivitis (red eye), corneal ulcers, nasal allergies, nasal tumors, collapsed nostrils (more common in flat-faced breeds), oral growths and

Keep your dog's ears dry, clean, and free of waxy buildup.

tumors, an incorrect bite, gum disease, collapsing trachea, ear flap infections, ear mites, ear tumors, partial or total deafness, and infections of the outer, middle, and inner ear.

Keep your dog's eyes, ears, nose, and mouth in good health by keeping these areas clean and dry and by checking them often for signs of a problem.

Bones and Joints

Your dog, even your little toy dog, has more bones than you do! All those bones and joints can sometimes cause your dog problems. Giant breeds can grow too fast and develop bones that aren't dense enough. Many large breeds are prone to degenerative hips, and many small breeds are prone to slipping kneecaps and elbows. Long-backed breeds are susceptible to ruptured spinal disks, and any breed can develop arthritis.

Signs that your dog is suffering from a bone or joint problem include:

• Limping or favoring a leg or paw

• Leg weakness or collapse

• Refusal or reluctance to move

• Yelping when touched

• Yelping after going up or down stairs, playing roughly, or jumping on or off a high surface such as a bed or couch

• Moving more slowly than usual

• Apparent fatigue

Is Your Dog CERF'd?

The Canine Eye Registration Foundation (CERF) keeps records of dogs screened for eye disorders like progressive retinal atrophy (PRA). When buying a puppy from a breeder, always ask if the parents of the litter have been CERF'd. Your breeder will know what you mean. If he doesn't, you would be well advised to find a different breeder, especially if PRA is a common problem in the breed that interests you.

Bone or joint problems will be evident in your dog's gait and movement.

Pain Management Side Effects

Dogs are particularly sensitive to the kinds of medications typically used for pain relief. While certain NSAIDs may protect against cartilage damage, some like aspirin actually contribute to it. Additionally, just as in humans, NSAIDS can cause side affects like intestinal bleeding and ulcers. When it comes to pain medication, more is *not* better! Never give your dog more pain medication than prescribed. You could seriously compromise your dog's health.

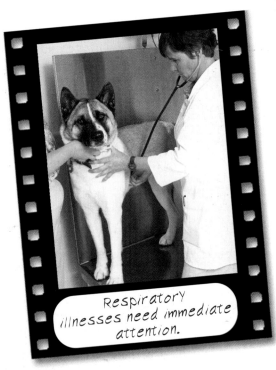

Respiratory illnesses need immediate attention.

Some of the more common musculoskeletal disorders include sprains, strains, and fractures; tendon injuries; dislocated joints; hip dysplasia (the most common cause of lameness in the back legs for dogs); Legg-Perthes disease (degeneration of the top of the leg bone, most common in toy breeds); luxating patella (slipped kneecap); elbow dysplasia (common cause of front-leg lameness, especially in large breeds); disk ruptures, especially in long-backed dogs like Dachshunds; various disorders common to rapidly growing large-breed puppies; osteoarthritis (degeneration of joints); and rheumatoid arthritis (an autoimmune disease).

Treatment for bone and joint disorders often consists of physical therapy, weight control (overweight aggravates orthopedic problems), surgery in extreme cases, pain relief with anti-inflammatory drugs or NSAIDs (non-steroidal anti-inflammatory drugs), and in cases of autoimmune diseases like rheumatoid arthritis, immunosuppressive drugs such as corticosteroids. Some conditions aren't curable but can be managed.

Respiratory System

Your dog's respiratory system consists of her nose, mouth, throat, and trachea, which bring air in and let air out, as well as her lungs and the muscles of her chest, which help to pump the air in and out. Obviously, respiration is essential for any living creature. Breathing supplies dogs with the oxygen they need and eliminates the carbon dioxide they don't need through exhalation, but breathing has another important function for dogs. Because dogs don't have as many sweat glands as humans, they must pant to keep themselves cool. That's part of how dog anatomy works.

Sometimes, your dog may actually have problems with respiration. Brachycephalic (flat-faced) dogs like Bulldogs, Pugs, Pekingese, Shih Tzu, Boxers, and Boston Terriers are more likely than other breeds to suffer from respiratory problems. Because their muzzles are short, air is cooled less efficiently, so these breeds become easily overheated. These breeds also sometimes suffer from congenital deformities that hinder breathing, like collapsed nostrils and an elongated soft palate. Keep brachycephalic dogs cool at all times and well supplied with fresh water to prevent heat stroke. A certain amount of snorting, snoring, and snuffling is natural for these breeds.

Dogs can also get laryngitis just like humans, from barking or coughing too much or due to a throat infection or tumor. Coughing is often a sign of a respiratory problem and can indicate a number of things.

Kennel cough complex is a highly contagious condition often spread around boarding kennels, the result of a number of different possible combinations of viruses and bacteria that cause coughing. A vaccinated dog will be resistant to many of the organisms that cause kennel cough complex, but any dog may contract this disease. Luckily, it isn't life threatening and dogs with good care and a low-stress environment usually recover quickly.

Breathing problems can signal other things, too, from a broken rib to an airway obstruction to heart failure. Always check with your vet if you notice that your dog is having trouble breathing.

Digestive System
The digestive tract is a long passageway through your dog's body with an important job: digesting food,

Do-It-Yourself Treatment for Vomiting and Diarrhea

If your dog is healthy, you can treat an episode of vomiting or diarrhea by withholding food and encouraging rest for your dog for approximately 12 hours. If the condition doesn't resolve in 24 hours, give your vet a call.

Part 3

Monitor your dog's eating habits and alert your vet to any significant changes.

taking the nutrients from the food and delivering it to the body, and eliminating the excess bulk as waste. Dogs have a sturdier digestive system than humans in that they can eat some things that would make a human sick. Dogs vomit easily and readily, which can quickly eliminate food that the digestive system won't accept.

However, dogs can suffer from many disorders of the digestive system, from ulcers to motion sickness to a foreign object in the intestine to bloat (also called gastric dilation volvulus), a serious and life-threatening veterinary emergency in which the stomach fills with air and twists.

Signs your dog is having a problem with her digestive system include:

- Vomiting

- Regurgitation

- Retching without vomiting

- Diarrhea

- Loss of appetite

- Sudden voracious appetite, especially without weight gain

- Excessive drooling

- Coughing

- Choking

- Gagging

- Unexplained weight loss or gain

- Bloating

Heartworm Alert

Heartworms can infect your dog, living and growing inside her heart. Untreated, heartworm can kill your dog, and treatment in the advanced stages is risky. Heartworms are spread by mosquitoes, so dogs that spend a lot of time outside are at greater risk. All dogs at risk for mosquito bites should be on heartworm preventive during mosquito season. Ask your vet to recommend a heartworm preventive and follow the directions carefully. *Your dog must be tested for the presence of heartworms before beginning heartworm preventive.*

Part 3

• Restlessness or pacing

• Pain upon defecation

• Stools mixed with blood and mucus

• Flatulence

• Sensitivity to the abdominal area

• Constipation

• Red, inflamed rectal area

• Dragging rear along the floor or ground during or after defecation

• Polyps

• Fistulas, or cysts around the rectum

• Yellowing of skin (sign of a liver problem)

• Frequent urination

• Excessive thirst

• Large appetite and weight loss together (may indicate diabetes)

• Symmetrical hair loss coupled with a pot-belly, fatigue, infertility, wasting, and weakness (could indicate Cushing's disease)

Coughing, gagging, and a cough that sounds like a goose honk (a sign of a condition called collapsing trachea, common in toy breeds) probably aren't emergencies either, unless your dog is actually choking on a foreign object. Treat constipation by making sure your dog drinks plenty of water and by adding fiber to her diet. Treat dragging rear along the floor

Canine Epilepsy

Epilepsy is a common nervous system disorder in many breeds that causes seizures. Grand mal seizures are short and during these seizures, a dog will collapse and his legs will become rigid, he will lose consciousness, then begin jerking and in some cases, drooling. Some dogs lose bladder and bowel control. Partial seizures usually involve jerking of just one part of the body. Other causes of seizures are encephalitis, a brain tumor or abscess, stroke, kidney or liver failure, heat stroke, poisoning, head injury, or a vaccination reaction.

Many circulatory problems are hereditary and can be controlled by your vet.

or other signs of that anal sacs need emptying by having your vet or groomer empty them (or do it yourself, but have your vet show you how, and don't expect it to be a pleasant experience).

Other signs of digestive problems warrant a call to your vet as soon as possible, and any sign of bloat–retching without vomiting, restlessness and pacing, and swelling of the stomach–should be treated as an emergency. Get your dog to the vet or veterinary emergency facility immediately. Always note any non-emergency digestive changes in your grooming journal so you can mention them to your vet at your next visit.

Circulatory System

Your dog's circulatory system is made up of his heart, veins, and capillaries. The heart pumps blood to all parts of the body, delivering nutrients and eliminating waste. When the heart doesn't work as well as it could, either through congenital abnormalities or heart disease that develops later in life, your dog can suffer from many serious and sometimes fatal conditions. Heart disease occurs in many breeds, from minor heart murmurs to life-threatening conditions such as cardiomyopathy, the most common cause of congestive heart failure in large dogs, and congenital heart defects such as valve malformations. The heart can also become infected by bacteria or secondarily inflamed due to other conditions like Lyme disease or distemper. Many dogs die from congestive heart failure.

Other types of circulatory problems include blood disorders like anemia, and clotting disorders like von Willebrand's disease (a bleeding disorder common in certain breeds) and hemophilia.

Signs your dog could have a circulatory or heart problem:

- Fatigue

- Weakness

- Bloated abdomen

- Coughing

- Weight loss

- Lethargy

- Rapid breathing

- Collapse

- Exercise intolerance

At your dog's annual checkup, your vet should check your dog's heart, but remember to report any symptoms that could indicate a heart or circulation problem.

Nervous System

Your dog's nervous system includes his brain, spinal cord, and nerves. This is information central for your dog, and damage or disease to the nervous system can result in serious neurological symptoms, like seizures, loss of control over bodily functions, senility, or paralysis. Dogs can suffer head and spinal injuries just like humans. The

Your Paraplegic Dog

Many dogs who become paralyzed in their rear legs due to a disk rupture or spinal accident go on to live long, happy lives with the help of wheeled carts that hold their hips up, allowing them freedom of movement. While people once commonly euthanized paralyzed dogs, today more owners are recognizing that paraplegic dogs can have a high quality of life free of pain and full of activity. While paraplegic dogs take a little extra care, they reward their owners many times over with their joyful affection and indomitable spirit.

If your dog has trouble walking or moving, take him to the vet immediately.

Part 3

Providing your dog with plenty of water will help to keep him healthy.

brain can become infected (encephalitis), can develop a tumor or abscess, or an arterial obstruction resulting in a stroke. Dogs can develop muscular dystrophy resulting in neurological symptoms and spinal cord degeneration (degenerative myelopathy) or sensory and motor nerve degeneration (called neuropathy). Senior dogs can even develop a condition similar to Alzheimer's disease.

Spinal cord conditions like disk ruptures, spinal tumors, spinal degeneration, spinal infection, and spinal bone spurs can cause pain, stiffness, weakness, or partial or total paralysis (temporary or permanent). Disk ruptures indicate a veterinary emergency because without surgery, they could result in permanent paralysis, typically of the rear legs. If your dog has a long back, particular common in Dachshunds but also in Basset Hounds, Beagles, Cocker Spaniels, Pekingese, and other long-backed dogs, and he shows any signs of a disk rupture, take him to your vet or veterinary emergency center immediately. While your vet may prescribe rest and medication instead of surgery, immediate treatment is essential for recovery.

Signs of a disk rupture include:

- Yelping after jumping up or down

- Yelping upon being patted on the head

- Refusal to walk up stairs or jump up onto couch, bed, or into a car

- Refusal to lower head to eat or drink

- Hunched position

- Panting, trembling

• Sudden reluctance to move

• Sudden reluctance to climb stairs

• Limping

• Depression, lethargy

Urinary System

Your dog's urinary system consists of the kidneys, bladder, urethra, and (in males) prostate. The urinary system is a crucial system for eliminating waste from your dog's body, and when it becomes damaged or diseased, your dog will not only suffer discomfort but could suffer serious or even fatal consequences.

Signs that something is wrong with your dog's urinary system include:

• Painful urination

• Red, inflamed, or swollen penis or vulva

• Excessive or insufficient urination

• Drinking more often

• Blood, mucus, or clots in urine

• Sudden inability to hold urine, sudden housetraining lapses

Kidney failure is a serious disease and can result in significant damage to the kidney. Dogs with kidney failure must be monitored closely by a vet and must be on a diet that restricts salt, protein, and phosphorous.

Signs of kidney failure include:

• Large urine output and excessive thirst

- Depression

- Weight loss

- Fatigue

- Loss of appetite

- Dry haircoat

- Brownish tongue

- Ammonia-like breath odor

Dogs can get kidney stones, bladder stones, and urinary tract and bladder infections, just like humans. They can also suffer from an enlarged or infected prostate and kidney failure.

Reproductive System

If you plan to breed your dog, you may encounter problems with the female's menstrual cycle, impotence in male dogs, reluctance to breed, false pregnancy, and any number of conditions that could result in fetal loss or malformation. Tutelage under an experienced and responsible breeder along with frequent veterinary visits can help you resolve these problems of breeding.

If you have a pet, let's hope you have already had him neutered. You may recall it was stated that having your dog neutered greatly decreases the risk of several reproductive cancers. While neutered dogs can suffer from reproductive system disorders, such as vaginitis (a vaginal infection) or endometritis (a bacterial infection of the uterus) in females or penile infection or a strictured foreskin in males, these are relatively uncommon for healthy dogs.

Spaying or neutering your dog will prevent many reproductive diseases.

Cancer

Cancer is one of the leading causes of death in pet dogs, and the leading cause of death in many breeds particularly susceptible to cancer. As pet owners have become more conscientious in caring for their pets, dogs are living longer and cancer–usually a disease of aging in pet dogs–seems to be on the rise. Whether it is simply diagnosed more often than before is unknown, but vets are seeing and treating canine cancers more frequently.

Cancer is the rapid growth of mutant cells that replace or overwhelm healthy tissue. Not all cancers show up as lumps or growths on your dog's skin, but because so many of them do, the annual veterinary exam is essential, especially for dogs over seven years old (considered the beginning of the "senior" years for the average dog). Internal tumors are harder to catch in their early stages, which is why behavioral changes in your dog like weight loss, fatigue, lethargy, and depression are important to mention to your vet, who can then do tests that may uncover cancer.

Because dogs can develop so many different kinds of cancers, anything unusual or any changes in your dog's skin should be noted, including sores that won't heal, and pigmented areas that could be melanomas or squamous cell carcinomas (skin cancers that may be caused by overexposure to the sun). Dogs can also get breast cancer, cancer of the reproductive organs (these cancers are rare in neutered dogs), bone cancer, and leukemia. Cancer is treated according to its type, and in the same manner as for humans, often involving the surgical

Blood tests can often determine any illnesses your dog may have.

But It Looks Like Cancer

Many growths and cysts on dogs are benign, such as those that often occur on the oil-producing sebaceous glands or those made of fat cells and fibrous tissue, but only a vet can tell you for sure, so point out any changes. If benign tumors interfere with a dog's movement, comfort ,or even his appearance, your vet may recommend they be removed unless the risk of the surgical removal is a greater risk to your dog than the tumor itself.

Part 3

removal of a tumor, radiation therapy, chemotherapy, immunotherapy, or a combination of these treatments.

Cancer warning signs include:

- Skin growths on the skin

- Warts

- Blood clots beneath the skin

- Growths, lumps, or nodules beneath the skin

- Unexplained sores

- Mole-like pigmented areas

- Red patches

- Cauliflower-like growths

- Enlarged lymph nodes

- Severe shortness of breath

- Anemia

- Bone growths

- Swollen limbs

- Abdominal mass

- Weight loss

• Vomiting

• Diarrhea

• Constipation

• Internal bleeding

More pet owners than ever before are electing to treat cancer rather than euthanize a dog with the disease, and many dogs live long, happy lives after treatment for cancer. Only you and your vet can decide how to manage cancer in your individual dog.

Holistic Health Care for Dogs

As more people become interested in holistic health for themselves, from herbal remedies and homeopathy to chiropractic care, acupuncture, and the natural foods movement, more and more pet owners are trying these therapies on their pets. The American Holistic Veterinary Medical Association (http://www.ahvma.org/index.html) has hundreds of member vets.

Holistic medicine approaches health care by looking at the big picture, including a patient's lifestyle, diet, health habits, hygiene, genetics, psychological state, relationships, and environment. Rather than focusing only on symptoms, holistic medicine treats the whole dog, person, or cat, or whoever the patient may be. Holistic health practitioners argue that treating symptoms only masks an underlying imbalance, and that this imbalance, not its symptoms, must be addressed for healing to occur. Imbalances are typically treated in the least invasive and least harmful method possible.

Good health care is important throughout your dog's life.

Pet Massage

A growing area of holistic health care for pets is pet massage. Practitioners of pet massage say it relaxes pets, helps them bond to humans, and can relieve muscle tension, pain, hypersensitivity, and even emotional conditions such as fear and anxiety. If the idea of pet massage interests you, ask your vet if she has heard of any pet massage practitioners in your area. Or, massage your dog yourself by gently kneading his skin starting at the head and face and working down the back, around the ribs, and down each leg. A pet massage is a great way to begin a weekly grooming session because it can also help you to identify any changes in your dog's skin, coat, and body.

Holistic health care and conventional medicine were once two different worlds, but as more people learn about what is best for their pets, more vets are embracing a complementary method, using the best of both worlds according to appropriateness. Acute situations such as broken limbs, trauma, severe infections, or emergency conditions like bloat are usually best treated with conventional medicine, but many people believe that chronic conditions like allergies, arthritis, hip dysplasia, and even certain cancers can be effectively treated using holistic methods.

Holistic health practices make sense for many pet owners because they focus on balance and prevention. When a dog gets sound nutrition, daily exercise, plenty of healthy human interaction, playtime, and training, that dog will be more likely to live a long, healthy life. When something does go wrong, holistic medicine seeks to balance the body to encourage self-healing.

Veterinary holistic medicine includes many different types of therapies. Some of them sound a little odd to those uninitiated into the realm of holistic health, and all have their detractors. However, thousands claim that their pets have benefited from holistic health therapies, which tend to be not only less invasive than many conventional medical treatments, but also less expensive.

The following are some of the more common techniques widely available to veterinary patients today.

Acupuncture and Acupressure

This ancient Chinese health therapy works to balance the body's energies and relieve pain by inserting needles or applying pressure to certain key places on the body thought to be energy meridians. Many pet owners claim their pets have become pain-free after a course of veterinary acupuncture or acupressure treatments.

Veterinary Chiropractic

Just as humans often visit chiropractors to help align, regulate, and treat musculoskeletal imbalances, veterinary chiropractors work on a dog's bones, joints, and muscles to align energy and adjust the spinal vertebra, restoring balance and allowing the body to heal itself without impediment.

Homeopathy

This 19th century invention by a German medical doctor operates on the principle that "like cures like." In other words, when a substance causes certain symptoms, then very minute and diluted doses of that same substance can alleviate those symptoms. For example, if a certain herb or bacteria causes severe headaches in large amounts, then tiny diluted amounts

Alternative or natural medicines are becoming popular in the treatment of dogs.

can cure a headache. Homeopathic practitioners claim that these remedies balance the body on its deepest vibrational level so that it can heal itself. Homeopathic remedies typically contain herbs, flowers, roots, minerals, viruses, bacteria, or animal-based ingredients. They are very safe because their active ingredients are so extremely diluted as to render them nontoxic, but should be used only under the direction of a homeopathic veterinarian.

Herbal Remedies

Veterinary herbalogists prescribe herbal remedies for pets as an alternative to conventional medications (although some conventional medicines are made from herbs, too). Just as with humans, please exercise caution using herbal remedies for pets. A trained veterinary herbalogist can prescribe appropriate herbal remedies for your dog, but don't try to do it yourself.

Check out the Veterinary Botanical Medicine Association on the Internet (http://www.vbma.org/) for more information about herbal remedies for pets.

Stop and Drink the Flowers

Flower remedies are substances made from purified water and flowers designed to balance a pet's emotional energies. They are typically added to your dog's water.

Part 3

First Aid

If your dog was hit by a car, in severe pain, attacked by another dog, or suffering from heat stroke, would you know what to do? Such thoughts aren't pleasant for anyone with a family pet, and reading a chapter like this can be stressful as you consider all the things that *could* happen, even if they never do.

However, even the healthiest of dogs can encounter an accident and knowing how to administer emergency first aid to your dog is essential for any pet owner. Better to be prepared than to be caught in an emergency without any idea what to do. Part of providing a healthy life for your pet is to be prepared in case of any emergency, even if you think the likelihood of a snakebite or poisoning or car

Curious puppies can get into all kinds of mischief.

What's the Best Medicine Again?

When it comes to emergencies, prevention is always best. Always keep your dog on a leash and supervised when out of the house and keep trash, poisons, choking hazards, and other dangers inaccessible. In the car, keep your dog confined, and never leave him in a car on a warm day, even with the windows cracked. Keep him safe from excessive cold and excessive heat, make sure he always has enough water, feed him regularly, and once again (and again and again), pay attention to your dog so you can catch any problems before they get too serious!

accident seem remote for your dog. This chapter will give you general guidelines for emergency care, but always defer to your vet's advice, and don't hesitate to call your vet or emergency veterinary clinic in the case of an emergency. Use this book to help you until you can get your dog to the vet.

Your Canine First Aid Kit

In an emergency, having the right supplies on hand immediately can mean the difference between life and death. Assemble a first aid kit designed just for your dog and keep it handy so you always know where to find it. Don't forget to bring it along when you take your dog in the car or especially on vacation.

Your first aid kit should include the following items inside a clearly labeled container that is easily portable, such as a nylon tote bag, plastic box, or backpack:

- Blanket or towel large enough to wrap up your dog or for use as a stretcher

- Nylon leash and collar

- Nylon, leather, or cage muzzle, in case you must treat your dog when he is injured and scared

- Digital rectal thermometer

- Package of gauze pads

- Gauze roll

- Adhesive tape (1-inch roll)

- Duct tape

• Small scissors for cutting tape and gauze

• Ace bandage

• Rubber tubing for a tourniquet

• Cotton swabs

• Cotton balls

• Tweezers

• Needle-nosed pliers

• Antihistamine tablets with dosage instructions attached for your dog's size (ask your vet ahead of time)

• Antibiotic ointment

• Hydrocortisone ointment

• Petroleum jelly

• Rubbing alcohol

• Hydrogen peroxide (to induce vomiting, not for wound cleaning)

• Surgical cleansing solution

• Saline eye wash

• Small flashlight or penlight

• Latex or plastic gloves

Part 3

• Eyedropper

• Grooming clippers (to remove hair from injured areas)

• Compressed activated charcoal with dosage instructions attached for your dog's size (ask your vet ahead of time)

• A card with emergency phone numbers, including:
  • Your vet, including address and directions to the office in case someone else has to drive or you are panicked and forget
  • Emergency after-hours vet clinic with address and directions
  • National Animal Poison Control Center: 800-548-2423 or 900-680-0000
  • Police or sheriff, in the case of an emergency involving another animal or person

Handling a Sick or Injured Dog: Safety First!

A sick, injured, or frightened dog does not behave like a happy, contented dog and can't be handled the same way. You must take certain precautions to make sure you don't injure your friend further and that you don't get injured yourself. Follow these guidelines for proper handling to keep everyone as safe as possible.

Muzzle Safety

If your dog is injured, frightened, or in great pain, he could bite you, even if he would never consider biting under normal circumstances. That would result in two emergencies instead of one! For this reason, a muzzle is an essential item in your emergency first aid kit.

However, misuse of a muzzle can spell disaster. Never use a muzzle that keeps your dog's mouth shut if he is having trouble breathing or if he is vomiting, wretching, choking, or unconscious. In these cases, a dog must be able to open his mouth or he could suffocate. A cage muzzle is a good option because it allows your dog to breathe through the

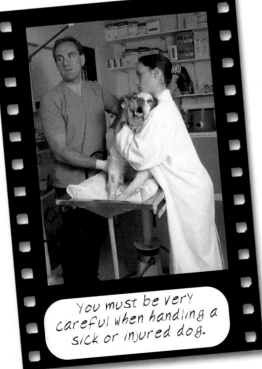

You must be very careful when handling a sick or injured dog.

mouth. When your dog's injuries don't involve breathing or vomiting, you can bind your dog's muzzle with a leash, a band of adhesive tape, or a nylon muzzle with a Velcro closure, handy for keeping your dog from biting while tending an injury or transporting to a vet. Other options are an Elizabethan collar or a No-Bite collar to keep your dog from turning his head to bite.

Moving and Transporting an Injured Dog

If you must move an injured dog, do so very carefully to avoid making injuries worse, especially if your dog has been hit by a car or doesn't move after jumping down from a high place, which could mean her spine is injured. Always transport a dog with suspected spinal injury on a stretcher. Gently slide your dog to the ground so he is lying on his side, if he isn't already, then gently slide him onto a flat surface like a piece of plywood, or even a large cutting board for a small dog.

A dog with a spinal injury should stay still, so if your dog is moving around a lot, secure a strip of duct tape over his shoulders and hips can keep him immobile. If you don't have a hard flat surface, use a towel or blanket as a makeshift stretcher. You may need someone else to hold the other side, depending on your dog's size.

If you must carry an injured dog in your arms, lift him correctly. Place one arm around his chest in front of his front legs, and the other arm under his rump, behind the rear legs, so that all four legs are between your two arms. Move him slowly and try not to move his spine.

Emergency Resuscitation and CPR

If your dog isn't breathing or if his heart has stopped, as could happen in the case of a heart attack, electrocution, drowning, or other accident or injury, you may have to

Safe Passage

Always move your sick or injured dog into a lying-down position on her side for transport. This position helps her to breathe more easily and is the least traumatic, especially if she is in shock or unconscious.

If your dog enjoys swimming, make sure you supervise him at all times.

perform emergency resuscitation and/or CPR on your dog. A dog that isn't breathing has no time to travel to a vet, although you can practice these steps while en route when someone else is able to drive you and your dog.

The first step is to determine your dog's condition.

- Is your dog breathing?

- If his chest is rising and falling, and/or if you can feel breath on your cheek, check his pulse.

- If he is not breathing, pull out his tongue and check to see if anything is obstructing the airway.

- If an object obstructs the airway, see if you can hook it out with your finger.

- If you can't, perform the Heimlich maneuver on your dog (see below).

- If you don't see airway obstruction, check for a pulse.

- Does your dog have a pulse?

- Feel for the large femoral artery on your dog's mid thigh.

- If he has a pulse but isn't breathing, begin mouth-to-nose resuscitation (discussed later in this chapter).

The Heimlich Maneuver

If your dog is choking on something–evident by gagging, distress, and pawing at the throat–but still breathing, get him immediately to the vet. If his airway is obstructed and he can't breathe, open your dog's mouth to look for a foreign object. Dogs have choked on many things, including pieces of rawhide, bone splinters, chew toys, and things they find in the trash. If you see something, try to hook it out of your dog's mouth with your finger, but be careful not to push the object further down into your dog's throat. If you can't easily remove the item, perform the Heimlich Maneuver.

Here's how:

• Put your dog on your lap with his back against your chest.

• Put your arms around your dog's waist and make a fist.

• Place your fist in the V at the bottom of your dog's rib cage, just above the abdominal cavity.

• Place your other hand over your fist, then forcefully thrust your fist upward four times quickly. This should force a burst of air through your dog's throat to dislodge the object.

Knowledge of first aid can save your dog's life.

• Sweep the object out with your finger.

• If the object does not dislodge, place your mouth over your dog's nose and force air with five quick breaths into his nostrils. Some air might get past the foreign object.

• Using the heel of your hand, strike your dog between the shoulder blades four times sharply to dislodge the object.

• Try the finger sweep again. If the object still won't dislodge, repeat these steps until your dog is breathing.

• When your dog is breathing again, take him immediately to the vet for follow-up care.

Emergency Breathing—Mouth-to-Nose Resucitation

Many emergency conditions can cause your dog to stop breathing, such as choking, electrocution, heart attack, a seizure, poisoning, or shock resulting from a trauma. If your dog isn't breathing, you don't have time to get to the vet without doing something. If you aren't comfortable learning emergency breathing by reading from a book, ask your vet to demonstrate the proper technique at your next visit.

Here's what to do:

1. Check to see if your dog has a heartbeat. If not, begin CPR (see below), which includes artificial breathing.

2. Pull your dog's tongue forward with your fingers, up to the level of the canine teeth.

3. For a small dog, place your mouth over your dog's nose, forming a seal around your dog's nostrils, and blow gently. For a large dog, also seal the dog's lips by placing your hand around the muzzle to prevent the escape of air.

4. Look for chest expansion. If the dog's chest doesn't expand, blow a little harder, until you see chest expansion.

5. Release your mouth after each breath, which will result in a natural exhalation and avoid over-inflation of your dog's lungs.

6. Continue, administering approximately one breath every two to three seconds (three seconds for larger dogs).

7. Continue until your dog begins to breathe on his own, or until the heartbeat stops.

8. If heartbeat stops, begin CPR.

CPR

If your dog has no heartbeat, you must begin CPR immediately. With a larger dog, CPR is easier with two people, but you can do it alone if necessary.

Here's what to do:

1. Put the dog on a flat surface on her right side. Place yourself behind the dog's back.

2. Cup your hands around a small dog's ribcage just behind the

CPR Safety

Never practice CPR or emergency breathing on a dog that doesn't need it. You could seriously injure a dog. Even if your dog does require CPR, it could cause broken ribs and other health complications, but these are less life-threatening than the situation requiring CPR, so administering the rescue technique is worth the risk.

elbows. For a puppy, use the fingertips of one hand and the thumb of the other hand. For large dogs, place the heel of your hand over the widest area of the rib cage, then place your other hand on top.

3. Compress your dog's chest to about 1/4 of the chest width by pushing your hands or fingertips together in the case of a small dog, or by pressing down with the heel of your hands on the ribcage of a larger dog. Compress or squeeze for 1 count, then release for 1 count, at about 100 compressions per minute for a small dog, about 80 compressions per minute for a large dog.

4. If someone is helping you, administer a breath as described above in the section on Emergency Breathing for every two to three compressions. If alone, administer a breath after every five compressions.

5. Continue until your dog is breathing and has a steady pulse. If your dog doesn't respond after ten minutes, chances are slim that he will recover.

What Do You Do If...

But, you may be thinking, how do I know when to administer CPR or emergency breathing, or when to use any of those things in the first aid kit? Many accidents can befall our pets, so consult this guide for advice on what to do when something happens. In an emergency situation, if your dog is in pain, distress, or is injured, you should *always* get to the vet as soon as possible, if you can. Sometimes there are things you can do first however, to help lessen the severity of the injury. Here's what to do if…

Your Dog Is Bleeding

If your dog has been injured and has a wound that is bleeding, the first thing to do is stop the bleeding and keep the area from becoming infected if possible. If a wound isn't bleeding because it has clotted, leave it alone and get to a

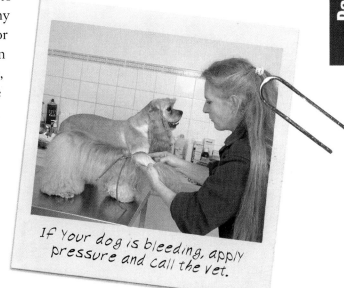

If your dog is bleeding, apply pressure and call the vet.

vet. However, if the wound is oozing or spurting blood, apply pressure.

Take several gauze pads from your emergency first aid kit and place them over the wound. Press with your finger or the heel of your hand (depending on the dog's size and the wound's size) for five to ten minutes. Secure the gauze with tape, adding more if necessary without removing the original gauze held against the wound. If you have bandaged the wound, watch for swelling, indicating the bandage is too tight. Loosen it but continue to apply pressure to the wound with your hand over the gauze.

Dogs may injure each other when fighting or playing.

If your dog is spurting blood from an artery and you can't stop the bleeding with pressure, apply a tourniquet. Only use a tourniquet if you can't control the bleeding with direct pressure. Place the tourniquet above the wound, or between the wound and the heart. With a strip of cloth or gauze, or even a belt, loop the tourniquet once or twice around the limb–again, above the wound–and insert a stick in the loop. Turn the stick to gently and slowly tighten the tourniquet. Tighten only to the point that bleeding stops. Loosen the tourniquet every ten minutes to prevent tissue death. Loosen the tourniquet and if blood continues to flow, let it flow for several seconds then retighten. If bleeding has stopped, apply a pressure bandage.

Once you have bleeding under control, transport your dog to the vet or emergency clinic, or work to stop bleeding while someone else drives you.

When bleeding is under control, if you can't get to a vet, you should clean the wound to prevent infection using the following procedure. If you can get to the vet, the following steps describe something similar to what your vet will do to clean and dress the wound:

1. Remove the dressing and clean the area around the wound (not the wound itself) with a surgical scrub like Betadine or Nolvasan.

2. Rinse the wound by squirting it with tap water using a large syringe, a commercial water

pik, a kitchen sink or bathtub sprayer, or an outdoor hose until the wound is completely clean. A vet will probably irrigate the wound using a diluted antiseptic solution.

3. If cleaning the wound yourself, cover with a fresh gauze pad after cleaning and rinsing, then take your dog to the vet as soon as possible.

4. A vet will remove dying tissue and foreign matter with a forceps and scissors or scalpel, but don't try to do this yourself.

5. Finally, a vet will close an open wound with tape or sutures. Infected or oozing wounds must first be treated, which could take several days of dressing changes.

6. In the case of a puncture wound, your vet may surgically enlarge and then repair the wound.

7. Finally, the wound will probably require bandaging to keep the area clean and protected. In the absence of vet care, bandage a clean wound yourself by applying gauze over the wound in several layers, then wrapping with elastic tape, tightly enough to keep the gauze in place but not so tight that it cuts off circulation. Watch for limb swelling as evidence of insufficient circulation and loosen dressing accordingly.

8. Follow wound-care, suture, and dressing directions from your vet. In the absence of vet care, change bandages every other day and watch for drainage, swelling, or signs of infection.

Your Dog Has Been Hit by a Car

If your dog is hit by a car, he could sustain broken bones, a damaged spinal cord, wounds and bleeding, shock, even a brain injury causing coma or seizures, or he might shake himself off and walk away. No matter how bad or how mild his injuries appear, take any dog hit by a car to a vet or emergency care clinic immediately.

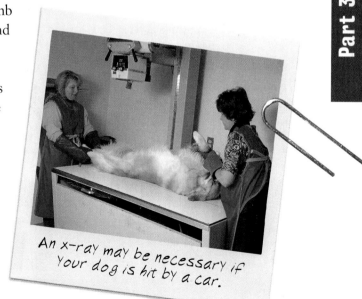

An x-ray may be necessary if your dog is hit by a car.

If your dog isn't breathing or has no heartbeat, follow the instructions above for emergency breathing or CPR. If he has bleeding wounds, follow the directions above to stop bleeding. If your dog is in shock but breathing, transport him lying on his side to the vet via a stretcher or blanket. Keep your dog calm by talking in a soft, gentle, soothing voice and reassure him. Stay with him and keep talking. If you are panicked and upset, it will probably make your dog more panicked and upset, too, possibly aggravating his condition.

Your Dog Has Been Attacked by an Animal

Dogs are often the victims of animal attacks, usually by other dogs but also by snakes and other wild animals like raccoons, rats, badgers, possums, and coyotes. Small dogs have been killed by owls, hawks, and eagles.

If your dog has been bitten by another mammal, suspect rabies. If another dog you don't know bites your dog, call the sheriff or police department immediately so they can arrange to apprehend the dog and confirm it doesn't have rabies. If you know the owner of the dog that bit your dog, confirm that dog has a rabies vaccination (ask to see the proof), or report the incident to the authorities so they can confirm.

Vaccinations will protect your dog from catching diseases from wild animals.

If a rodent, raccoon, bat, or other wild animal bites your dog, you probably won't be able to relocate the animal for testing. *Don't touch a wild animal or try to catch it yourself.* Humans can get rabies, too. Get your dog to the vet and tell him that your dog was bitten.

If a poisonous snake bites your dog, keep your dog quiet and calm to slow the spread of venom. Do not wash or touch the wound, apply ice, or make any cuts. Do not attempt to suck out the venom. These treatments don't work and could injure your dog further or even injure you. Get your dog to an emergency facility as soon as possible for treatment with antihistamines, antivenin if available, and respiratory, circulatory, and intravenous fluid support. If your dog was bitten by a poisonous snake but isn't showing signs, take him to the vet nevertheless, as some venoms don't cause symptoms immediately.

If you didn't see the attack but suspect a poisonous snake, look for the following signs:

- One or two puncture wounds

- Severe pain

- Swollen, discolored tissue

- Panting and drooling

- Vomiting

- Diarrhea

- Neurological symptoms such as sudden lack of coordination, seizures, twitching

- Sudden weakness

- Extreme restlessness

- Slowed breathing

- Pinpoint pupils

- Shock

Dog Eat Dog

Many dogs are naturally dog-aggressive, even those who would never think of biting a human. Small dogs are at risk for severe injury from attacks by larger dogs, but large dogs, particularly of the same sex and, in the case of males, those that are unneutered, are likely to squabble. Depending on the breed and the individual, squabbles can result in serious injuries. If all involved dogs are vaccinated for rabies, treat wounds as for any other injury.

Depending on the severity of the bite and the size and health of the dog, symptoms may be nonexistent, mild, or extreme. Sometimes even with veterinary care, the bite will be fatal, but the sooner your dog is treated, the better her chances for recovery.

Your Dog Is Drowning

Dogs are natural swimmers, but that doesn't mean they can't drown if they fall through ice, are swept away by a current or floodwaters, or if they are unable to get out of a swimming pool or lake. After removing a dog from the water, immediately hold him

Although dogs are natural swimmers, you need to be cautious around water.

upside-down by the chest or rear legs to help excess water run out of his nose and mouth. Check for breathing and heartbeat, and administer emergency breathing or CPR as indicated in those sections earlier in this chapter.

Your Dog Has Been Electrocuted

Puppies are notorious for chewing on electrical cords, but older dogs can also be electrocuted if they come into contact with a downed power line or are hit by lightning, or even if they are in the vicinity of a lightning strike.

Never touch a dog in contact with an electric cord, or you could also be electrocuted. Shut off power, pull the plug, and then check for breathing and heartbeat. If either of these is absent, administer emergency breathing or CPR as described in those sections earlier in this chapter. If your dog is conscious and breathing, take her to the vet to check for heart damage, pulmonary damage, mouth burns, or neurological damage.

You Think Your Dog is Poisoned

A dog's world is filled with potential poisons: pest poisons, antifreeze, human medications, overdoses of pet medications, garbage, chocolate, household cleaners and chemicals, even poisonous plants in your home or garden. Treatment for poisoning is much more effective if your vet knows the kind of poison your dog ingested. If possible, bring the bottle, box, or container of any poison your dog has ingested with you to the vet.

Getting poison out of your dog's system as soon as possible is crucial, but in the case of some poisons, vomiting can cause even more harm. If you know your dog has ingested a particular poison and your vet or poison control center advises vomiting, induce vomiting by giving your dog a 3-percent hydrogen peroxide solution. Give 1 teaspoon per 10 pounds of body weight every 15 to 20 minutes, no more than 3 times, until the dog vomits.

Always induce vomiting if you know your dog has swallowed an overdose of his medication or has gobbled human medication like acetaminophen, ibuprofen, diet pills, sleeping pills, heart pills, blood pressure pills, antihistamines, vitamins, or any other medication not specifically prescribed for your dog.

After your dog vomits, give him activated charcoal to bind remaining poison and keep it from damaging your dog. Keep 5-gram tablets of compressed activated charcoal in your emergency first aid kit. Administer one tablet per ten pounds of body weight. Tablets are the easiest form of activated charcoal to administer to your dog. Alternatively, give your dog one-quarter cup egg white mixed with one-quarter cup milk per ten pounds of body weight, administered with a plastic syringe into your dog's cheek.

> ### Poison Alert
>
> The most common cause of poisoning in pets is from an overdose of medication prescribed for a pet, or from the ingestion of human medication.

If your dog has ingested an acid, alkali, cleaning solution, household chemical, or petroleum product, *do not induce vomiting!* Seek medical treatment immediately. Rinse out your dog's mouth and give him water or milk to dilute the poison.

Other signs you should not induce vomiting are:

• If your dog is showing neurological symptoms like seizures, convulsions, or an unsteady gait.

• If your dog has ingested a product that says "Do not induce vomiting" on the label.

• If your dog is unconscious or having trouble breathing.

• If your dog has swallowed a sharp object such as a bone fragment.

• If your dog has already vomited.

If your dog ingests a poison intended for pests, either in the house (roaches, ants, mice, rats) or in the yard (gophers, moles, etc.), immediately induce vomiting except as indicated above.

If you suspect your dog has eaten something harmful, call poison control and your vet.

Dangerous Indoor & Outdoor Plants

Some of the more common indoor plants that are poisonous include the following (this is a partial list—many other houseplants can cause poisoning):

Amaryllis	Dieffenbachia (dumbcane)
Asparagus fern	Elephant's Ear
Azalea	Ivy (many types)
Bird-of-paradise	Mother-in-law plant
Boston ivy	Nightshade
Caladium	Philodendron
Chrysanthemum (mums)	Poinsettia
Creeping Charlie	Tuberous begonia
Crown of thorns	Umbrella plant

Many different outdoor plants can cause poisoning, from mild to severe. Ask your vet what plants in your area are toxic, since outdoor plants vary widely according to geographical location. Some of the more common and ubiquitous outdoor plants that can cause poisoning in your dog include the following (this is a partial list—many other plants can cause poisoning):

Almond tree	Mushrooms
Azalea	Peach tree
Castor bean	Periwinkle
Cherry tree	Poppies
Daffodil	Potatoes
Delphinium	Rhododendron
English holly	Rhubarb
Foxglove	Spinach
Jimsonweed	Apricot
Lupine	Tomato vines
May apple	Wild Cherry
Mock orange	Wisteria
Morning glory	

Antifreeze poisoning is common in dogs because antifreeze often leaks from car radiators and it tastes sweet. Pet owners may not be aware they have a puddle of antifreeze in their garage until the dog starts sniffing with interest. Three ounces of antifreeze can kill a 40-pound dog. Symptoms of antifreeze poisoning occur 30 minutes to 12 hours after ingestion and include vomiting, "drunken" behavior, depressed behavior, and coma. Dogs often die from antifreeze poisoning, and those that seem to recover may develop kidney failure within a few days.

Induce vomiting immediately if your dog has ingested even a small amount of antifreeze, then take your dog to the vet without delay. Activated charcoal can help to keep your dog's system from absorbing the poison. Some brands of antifreeze are made with propylene glycol instead of the highly toxic ethylene glycol. While these products are also toxic, they are supposedly less likely to cause death.

If your dog is poisoned by a plant, symptoms can range from mouth irritation and vomiting to coma and sudden death. While some dogs would never think to eat a plant, some dogs, particularly puppies, are likely to chew on just about anything, especially when they aren't supervised. If you have a dog, be aware of which plants are poisonous and which are benign, and if you have a chewer, deny access to potentially poisonous plants.

Your Dog Has Heat Stroke and/or Dehydration

A dog exposed to high heat can experience a dangerous rise in body temperature. Dogs don't handle heat as well as humans, particularly dogs with short, flat faces and with long heavy coats with

Dogs are Not Kids

Many parents have syrup of ipecac in the medicine cabinet to induce vomiting in children who have ingested poison, and this remedy was once commonly prescribed for dogs, too. However, hydrogen peroxide is more effective and safer for dogs than syrup of ipecac, which should be avoided unless your vet specifically advises it.

Many plants in your yard can be poisonous to your dog.

Heatstroke Prevention

Prevent heatstroke by never leaving your dog in a car even when you don't think it's very hot, especially when the sun is out. Also don't let your short-faced dog spend too much time in hot humid weather, restrict exercise in severe heat, and make sure your dog always has plenty of cool, fresh water.

Make sure your dog has plenty of cool water and shelter on hot days.

origins in arctic climates. Dogs often suffer heatstroke when they are left inside cars in warm weather because the temperature inside a car can rise quickly compared to the temperature outside, particularly on a sunny day. Dogs also may experience heatstroke if they exercise too much when the weather is hot and humid, or if they are muzzled while under a dryer at the groomer's. Dogs confined in small warm areas without proper ventilation, on hot surfaces like concrete, or who suffer from a fever due to illness may also suffer from heatstroke.

Signs of heat stroke include heavy panting, labored breathing, a bright red tongue and mouth, thick saliva, and vomiting. Rectal temperature can rise to 104 to 110 degrees Fahrenheit. The dog may have bloody diarrhea, go into shock, or suffer collapse, seizure, coma, and death.

Dogs suffering from heatstroke must be cooled quickly. Bring the dog into a cool place such as an air-conditioned building or at least in the shade on a cool surface. Spray the dog with a hose (make sure the water is cool, not hot, if the hose has been in the sun), or immerse him in a tub of cool water. Put a wet dog in front of a fan and monitor rectal temperature every 10 minutes until it reaches 103 degrees Fahrenheit. At this point, dry the dog and stop cooling him to prevent hypothermia or shock.

Sometimes a dog with heatstroke is also dehydrated, but dogs can also become dehydrated after an episode of vomiting and/or diarrhea. Dehydration can cause subsequent heatstroke.

Signs of dehydration include loss of skin elasticity, dry mouth, dry gums, thick saliva, sunken eyes, collapse, and shock. If you think your dog is dehydrated, take him to the vet or

Warm Your Dog Safely

If your dog has hypothermia, do not treat him by dunking him into a hot bath or warming him with a blow-dryer, as these could cause tissue damage. Instead, warm your dog gradually with warm compresses and gentle handling.

Although your dog enjoys the outdoors, he should always have access to your home.

emergency vet clinic immediately for intravenous fluid replacement.

If your dog is only mildly dehydrated and isn't vomiting, use a squirt bottle or syringe to give her an electrolyte solution made for children. Give your dog about 2 to 4 mL per pound of body weight every hour.

Your Dog Has Hypothermia or Frostbite

A dog left outside in cold weather for too long can suffer from hypothermia, a dangerous drop in body temperature. Dogs with short coats, very young or very old dogs, and dogs that get wet in the cold are particularly susceptible to hypothermia.

Suspect hypothermia if your dog is shivering, listless, lethargic, has a weak pulse, and has a temperature lower than 95 degrees Fahrenheit. Hypothermic dogs may be revived after longer periods without heartbeat or breathing. A hypothermic dog must be gradually warmed. Wrap him in a blanket and take him inside a warm place. Dry him well with towels if he is wet. Encourage the dog to drink water with sugar or honey dissolved in it. If your dog's temperature is below 95 degrees, call your vet for instructions and apply warm water bottles wrapped in towels to your dog's chest. Continue until rectal temperature reaches 100 degrees F.

Part 3

Suspect frostbite, particularly common on tails, tips of ears, pads of feet, and the scrotum, if skin in these areas is very pale or blue and becomes swollen and red upon warming, then sometimes black. Frostbitten tissue dies and will peel or fall away within a few weeks. Apply warm water to frostbitten tissue until color returns. Do not use hot water or hot air, and never rub frostbitten tissue, as this causes tissue damage. Frostbite can be very painful. Restrain a dog that becomes upset or tries to irritate a frostbitten area, and see your vet for further treatment.

Your Dog Has Been Burned

Dogs can be burned in many ways: by electrocution, the sun, a hot surface, a hot liquid, or corrosive chemicals. If your dog is burned, see a vet immediately. Burns require professional attention to protect skin, and large burns may induce shock and require secondary treatment for infection and fluid loss.

For a small, superficial burn, apply a cool cloth (not ice) to the area for 20 minutes to minimize injury and for pain relief. Clip hair from the burn, wash skin gently with an antiseptic solution, and apply antibiotic ointment. Bandage carefully and change the dressing daily, reapplying antibiotic ointment with every dressing change.

Chemical burns should be flushed with water for ten minutes before dressing and blotted dry, and should be checked by a vet. Wear gloves when treating chemical burns to prevent getting burned yourself.

Your Dog Is in Shock

Shock is a condition caused by trauma in which the body's circulatory and respiratory systems slow drastically, causing a lack of sufficient oxygen and blood flow to the body. This is an emergency condition requiring immediate medical attention. Suspect your dog is going into shock if he has suffered a trauma, such as a heart attack, severe accident, allergic reaction, or poisoning, and begins to pant, suffer an increased heart rate, and has bright red mouth and tongue. Advanced shock is evident by pale skin and gums; cold extremities; lowered body temperature, heart rate, pulse, and respiration rate; lethargy; and loss of consciousness or coma.

If your dog isn't breathing or has no heart rate, administer emergency breathing or CPR, as described earlier in this chapter. Control bleeding of any wounds, and, if possible, splint

Anaphylactic Shock

Shock is caused by trauma, but anaphylactic shock is a specific allergic reaction to such things as penicillin, insect venom, or a vaccination. Signs of anaphylactic shock include a skin reaction at the sting or vaccination site, as well as general signs of shock such as diarrhea, vomiting, labored breathing, a swollen throat, weakness, severe restlessness, collapse, and coma. Without treatment, dogs can quickly die from anaphylactic shock, so transport your dog to a vet immediately.

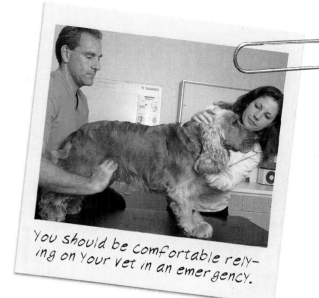

You should be comfortable relying on your vet in an emergency.

or stabilize broken bones as described earlier in the chapter.
Rest your dog on his right side and using a stretcher or blanket, take him immediately to a vet or emergency vet clinic.

During the course of treatment and transport, stay calm and talk in a gentle soothing manner to your dog. Even if she doesn't appear to be conscious, she may be affected by your behavior. Fear and anxiety could worsen her condition.

Your Dog Has a Broken Limb

If your dog is hit by a car or jumps or falls from a great height, or if you have a toy breed puppy that jumps out of someone's arms or is accidentally stepped on, suspect a broken bone. Signs of a bone fracture include a misshaped limb, swelling, redness, pain, lameness, or in the case of a compound fracture, bone protruding through skin. Fractures can result in dangerous blood loss, damage to internal organs, and shock. Dogs in extreme pain may be likely to bite, so use a muzzle if necessary.

Clean any open wounds and splint bones in their broken position for transport to your vet. Do not attempt to straighten a broken bone before splinting. Leave this to your vet. Splinting or securing broken limbs are to prevent further damage in transport, not for the purpose of healing the fracture.

Part 3

An injury to your dog's eyes requires quick medical care.

Eyeball Relocation

If you can't get to an emergency facility within 30 minutes, you may have to relocate the eyeball yourself. You need two people for this job. As one person restrains the dog, the other person should lubricate the eye socket with petroleum jelly and lift the eyelid out and over the eyeball while putting gentle pressure on the eyeball with moist cotton to slip the eyeball back into the socket. If you can't do it yourself right away, go to a vet or emergency clinic. Your dog is likely to lose vision, but with treatment, the condition is not fatal.

Splint lower-limb fractures using a folded newspaper or thick piece of cardboard secured to the limb with gauze or tape. Upper-limb, spinal, head, or torso fractures are best handled by immobilizing the dog during transport, such as by duct tape and a stretcher as described earlier in this chapter, or by keeping the dog calm and still.

Your Dog Has an Eye Injury

If your dog's eye is injured or if he loses an eye (this sometimes happens in breeds with protruding eyes like Pekingese, Pugs, Maltese, and Boston Terriers), you must act quickly. A traumatized dog can sometimes strain so hard that its eye bulges out to the point that it becomes dislocated. Swelling in the eye socket makes relocation of the eyeball difficult, so time is of the essence. Get to the closest emergency facility right away. Carry the dog, eye covered with a wet cloth, and keep the dog from bothering the eye socket.

Your Dog Is in Pain and You Don't Know Why

Sometimes you know your dog is in distress but you have no idea why because you didn't see what happened or because there is no obvious explanation. When your dog is in pain,

Part 3

call your vet and describe the symptoms or take her to an emergency clinic. Remember to stay calm, be soothing, and reassure her that you are there to take care of her.

It's frustrating to have a suffering pet and not know the reason why, but the way you respond to emergency situations will often directly impact how your dog responds, so be the responsible caretaker and stay calm, act quickly and rationally, and do everything you can to ease your pet's anxiety and pain.

Part 3

Your Healthy Senior Dog

After the challenges of puppyhood and the happy equilibrium of adulthood, dogs, like people, enter those golden years. The average age for re-evaluating your dog's care and granting her senior status is seven years, but dogs vary in their expected lifespan almost as much as they vary in size. The smaller the dog, the longer it is likely to live. While a Great Dane is heading into senior status at age five or six, a Chihuahua is just barely ending his adolescence. Large and giant breeds like Newfoundlands, Bloodhounds, Irish Wolfhounds, and Mastiffs are lucky to make it to age 11 or 12, but toy breeds often make it to 19 or 20 years old, some even older. Experts say the maximum canine lifespan is probably about 27 years, but few dogs ever make it to that age.

As your dog ages, he will need more of your time and attention.

Lifespan vs. Size

The average life expectancy of pet dogs is approximately 13 years, but large breeds typically live 10 to 12 years, and toy dogs typically live to 15 or 16 years.

Just because your dog is getting old doesn't mean you must suddenly cut her calories, change her food, or force her to "take it easy" (your grandma doesn't like that either!). But, entering the senior stage of life does necessitate a heightened vigilance about changes in your dog's body and behavior. Diseases like cancer, heart disease, diabetes, and many other conditions become more common with age in both dogs and people, so paying closer attention and increasing those annual vet visits to once every six months can ensure that your dog can live as long as possible.

The Signs of Canine Aging

When your dog gets older, his body doesn't work quite as well as it once did. He may not see, hear, smell, or taste as well as he once did. When your dog can't see or hear as well, he may become more irritable or nervous because he isn't as aware of what is going on around him. A touch from behind could startle him. Strangers might seem more threatening if he hasn't detected their approach. He may become more likely to guard his food.

Your dog may slow down in his senior years.

Your dog may also lose control over some of his functions. He may begin to have occasional housetraining accidents, lose control of his back legs, suffer respiratory problems and fatigue that could indicate heart disease (or other diseases), or his digestive system may become more sensitive. He may even get disoriented or suffer other signs of senility.

Depending on the dog, the breed, the size, and the age, functional decline can begin anywhere from 5 years to 15 years. Depending on what happens to your dog, you can make changes in his lifestyle and care to head off serious health problems and to make him feel more comfortable and secure. If your older dog starts showing age-related changes, talk to your vet about increasing annual exams to twice a year and make a note to let your vet know about the changes you've noticed so she can do

Part 3

the appropriate examinations and tests. Many of these symptoms of age-related decline or disease are the same as symptoms to watch for in younger dogs developing a disease, but they become more likely to occur as a dog ages.

Remember that some signs of aging are inevitable as a dog's body ages, such as slight decreases in activity, less energy, and decreased sharpness of vision and hearing. Conditions like age-related deafness may be incurable, but many symptoms signify diseases and other conditions that can be treated and are not inevitable with age. Seek veterinary advice and care for any of the following:

- Sudden exercise intolerance

- Weakness

- Unusual fatigue

- Rapid breathing or difficulty breathing

- Wheezing or panting

- Increase in thirst and frequency of urination

- Changes in bowel habits including diarrhea or constipation

- Loss of appetite

- Weight loss

- Coughing

The Nutraceutical Option

Herbal remedies, certain vitamins, and other substances called nutraceuticals that are not quite food but not quite vitamins are gaining in popularity for both dogs and humans as a preventive or treatment for certain chronic conditions like arthritis and digestive disorders. Many new dog food formulations include these ingredients, such as glucosamine and chondroitin sulfate to protect and maintain joint cartilage and probiotics to improve digestive function. These nutraceuticals can also be purchased in supplement form.

Part 3

• Bloody or pus-filled discharge from any orifice

• Increased pulse

• Increased temperature

• Lumps, nodules, or growths anywhere on the body

• Disorientation, failure to recognize familiar people, seeming to get lost in the house

• Cloudy eyes or other signs of vision loss

• Swollen gums and/or lost teeth

Preventive Geriatric Care

The most important thing you can do to ensure that your dog's senior years are healthy is to practice good health care throughout your dog's puppyhood and adult years. A healthy young dog is more likely to be a healthy old dog.

Your dog's coat will go through many changes as he matures.

Once your dog is a senior, however, you can make certain changes in her routine and care to help keep her as healthy and comfortable as possible.

Aging Skin and Coat

As your dog ages, his skin becomes less supple and his coat becomes drier. He is also more likely to develop tumors, nodules, cysts, and sores on his aging skin. Increase your weekly grooming exam to every other day or even daily for your senior dog, rather than every week. Not only will your dog enjoy the added attention and handling from you, but you will be more likely to find skin changes that you can show your vet. If a bump turns out to be an infection or even a cancer, you'll find it early and increase the chances of effective treatment.

More frequent brushing will also help to keep your dog's coat healthier by distributing oils. A moisturizing coat conditioner or spray can help to keep the coat shiny, too. Just because your dog is old doesn't mean he can't look and feel good.

Weight Management

Because older dogs tend to be achier and less interested in exercise, they also tend to require fewer calories. However, pampering owners may be inclined to feed their aging dogs even more food, just because they think their older dogs need to have something to enjoy. Nothing could be more dangerous for your aging pet! Obesity is not only the most common nutrition-related disease of adult dogs, but also one of the most common health conditions of older dogs. Obesity aggravates many other conditions of aging, like arthritis, heart disease, and diabetes. Your achy pet will be even achier if he is carrying around extra weight. Joints will deteriorate faster, muscles will grow weaker, the heart will have to work harder, exercise will become more uncomfortable, and your dog will decline more quickly. Overweight dogs are more likely to succumb to the diseases of aging faster and they may indeed live shorter lives.

Adjust the brand of food to fit your senior dog's needs.

Feed your dog according to her activity level. Some seniors stay very active to the end of their lives, but those who slow down don't need as much food. If you notice your dog's shape is changing, that nice waist tuck is disappearing, those ribs are becoming impossible to find, then decrease your dog's food intake. Cutting down on treats may be all that is required.

If your dog seems to be gaining weight inexplicably, talk to your vet because this could indicate a medical problem. Stomach bloating could also be due to a tumor.

The bottom line is that the two most important keys to keeping your senior dog (or anyone) at a healthy weight are to make sure he gets daily moderate exercise and a healthy diet in an appropriate number of calories. Your senior dog needs approximately 30 calories

Senior Kibble?

Your dog is seven. Should you switch to that food in the pet store labeled "Senior Formula"? Not necessarily. If your dog is still active and doing well on her food, you have no reason to switch formulas. If your dog is less active than she once was, you should decrease the number of calories she consumes each day, but not necessarily the type of food. Senior formulas typically have fewer calories and more fiber, which can add bulk to your dog's diet and help her feel less hungry on fewer calories. But look at the protein content. Senior formulas with reduced protein aren't a good idea for aging dogs that may need more protein to fight muscle atrophy. The one exception: dogs with kidney or liver disease do need low-protein diets, as prescribed by a vet.

Regular checkups are important to maintain good health.

per pound of body weight, more (35 to 40) if he is very active and a little less (25) if he is very sedentary. Check your dog food label for calorie content or estimate that dry kibble has about 1,600 calories per pound, canned about 500 calories per pound. Then, adjust according to whether your dog does well on the diet. Hunger is not an indication that he isn't getting enough calories. Instead, monitor his appearance and energy level. If you are unsure about how much to feed your senior dog, check with your vet for a personalized recommendation.

Arthritis and Aging Muscles

As bones, joints, and muscles age, they experience wear and tear. Joints become stiffer and more painful, and muscles become weaker and less flexible. You may have heard that exercise and weight lifting is important for aging humans to fight the age-related decline of muscles, bones, and joints. Older dogs also benefit immensely from regular exercise, which helps keep muscles toned and joints freer. Pay attention to how your

Part 3

Genetic Test Certification

The Orthopedic Foundation for Animals (OFA) keeps records of genetic tests done on purebred dogs so that breeders can register their dogs as certified free of hip dysplasia, elbow dysplasia, autoimmune thyroiditis, congenital cardiac disease, or patella luxation. OFA also tracks abnormalities based on DNA testing that indicate other conditions specific to certain breeds, like progressive retinal atrophy and von Willebrand's disease. A breeder should be able to show you proof that the parents of a litter of puppies have been certified free of hip dysplasia and other diseases or conditions to which a particular breed may be prone. However, parents certified free of hip dysplasia or other inherited conditions does not guarantee that your dog won't develop those conditions later in life. For more information on certification against certain inherited diseases, visit OFA's website at www.offa.org.

dog tolerates exercise, however. Don't push her to the point of pain. Your vet can prescribe medication for a dog with arthritis, but exercise is equally important.

Hip dysplasia also occurs with greater frequency in older dogs, especially in larger breeds. Large dogs fed too many calories as puppies are even more prone to the disease, and if your dog experiences weakness, pain, or loss of function in his legs or hips, ask your vet about the possibility of dysplasia. A dog with mild dysplasia may not require any treatment, but more serious cases typically require pain relief in the form of NSAID analgesics, medication to relieve joint inflammation and repair cartilage, restriction of certain activities like running and jumping (while still maintaining and exercise regimen including non-stressful activities like swimming and walking), and in extreme cases, surgery, ranging from simple repositioning of hips or removal of certain muscles to a total hip replacement.

Long in the Tooth, Sore in the Gums

Good dental care throughout life is important for keeping teeth and gums healthy in older dogs, but even so, older dogs may need their

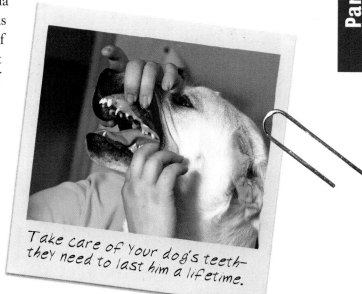

Take care of your dog's teeth—they need to last him a lifetime.

teeth cleaned more often than younger dogs. If you've never had your dog's teeth professionally scaled by a vet, this procedure may become necessary later in life. Some individual dogs require cleaning more than others, as they seem to accumulate more tartar. Gums in older dogs may become infected and can lead to pain, tooth loss, and difficulty eating, which can debilitate an old dog quickly. Oral bacteria and infection can travel to the heart, so good dental hygiene is more than a matter of aesthetics.

Check your senior dog's teeth every day and keep them well brushed, especially if your dog can no longer chew on hard biscuits. Have your vet look over teeth and gums closely and scale them if necessary at least twice a year. This should be part of the regular checkup, but remember to mention any oral changes or signs that your dog is experiencing dental or periodontal pain.

Cognitive Dysfunction Syndrome

When your dog ages, her brain ages, too, in a variety of ways. Plaque deposited in the brain can cause cell death and brain shrinkage. Aging brains have lower oxygen levels and experience changes in certain neurotransmitters like serotonin, norepinephrine, and dopamine. The result is a decline in brain function manifesting as senility. This disease is similar to Alzheimer's disease in humans, and about half of senior dogs over age ten will probably exhibit some symptoms to varying degrees.

Recently, veterinary medicine has discovered ways to improve the symptoms of cognitive dysfunction syndrome through medication. See your vet if your dog experiences any of the following signs of age-related neurological decline:

- Disorientation

- Getting lost or "stuck" in familiar areas like the house or yard

- Failure to recognize familiar people or respond to familiar verbal cues

- Changes in sleep habits

- Strange behaviors like circling, shaking, weakness, or aimless wandering

Safety for Senile Dogs

A dog suffering from cognitive dysfunction syndrome could easily become lost if he wanders out of the house or yard. While all dogs should be kept safely confined, senile dogs require particular vigilance because they may not be able to find their way back. This is of particular concern for dogs who always stick close to home and whose owners have never had to worry about keeping them on a leash or within a fence, because they may be less accustomed to being careful to keep their pets confined. Remember, a senile dog may want to come home but may be unable to, even if he is only a short distance away. Keep your aging pet safe.

Make sure your dog has proper identification in case he becomes lost.

• Housetraining accidents that can't be attributed to other health problems

• Showing little or no interest in family members

• Increasing failure to greet people when they come home (could also be a sign of hearing loss)

• Showing little or no interest in activities once enjoyed like petting, playing, chasing, or retrieving (could also be related to arthritis or other movement-induced pain)

Testing for Better Health

As recommended above, senior dogs can be better assured of proper care if they have a physical exam by a vet twice a year instead of just once a year. During the physical exam for a senior dog, your vet may decide that certain tests are required, based on symptoms that you've mentioned or changes that she notices. While more tests cost more money, they are also an invaluable tool for catching diseases in the early stages, and they could significantly extend your dog's lifespan and life quality if they give your vet the information she needs to treat a developing health problem.

Part 3

Your senior dog needs your love and patience more than ever.

During a checkup for a senior dog, your vet should give your dog a thorough physical exam to look for skin changes, lumps and bumps, and any infections, parasites, or painful areas. She will also do a complete blood workup and an urinalysis. Your vet should check your dog's teeth and clean and scale them if necessary (you may need to schedule a separate appointment for this procedure). Also, if your dog is experiencing certain symptoms of liver, kidney, or heart disease, your vet may decide to do liver and kidney function tests, a chest X-ray, or an electrocardiogram.

Your Senior Dog's Special Needs

Your senior dog has a few other special needs beyond scheduling more frequent vet check-ups and grooming. As your dog ages, his senses dull, and his body doesn't work as well, he may become more irritable, more confused, and more in need of comfort, assistance, and reassurance. It isn't easy getting old, and your dog may become startled more easily, behave more irritably, or be reluctant to do the things he used to do because he is achy and sore or because he doesn't understand why he can't move the way he used to move. Try to protect him from situations that will put him under extra stress if he isn't feeling well, such as subjecting him to lots of chaos, small children that want to poke and prod, or unnecessary time away from you.

To make your dog feel more comfortable and safer in his old age, make an effort to spend a little more quiet time together. Take him on a daily walk, but don't push the pace beyond what he can handle. Be patient with your dog and let him have his space when he needs it.

If your dog has a hard time getting around due to hip dysplasia, disk disease, or arthritis, make things easier. A carpet-covered board can serve as a ramp up to your small dog's favorite chair or the bed, if your dog sleeps with you. Rearrange food and water bowls to minimize trips up and down the stairs.

Part 3

As throughout your dog's youth and adulthood, vigilance is the best way to determine what your dog really needs. Just because your dog is aging doesn't mean he can't continue to exercise vigorously. If your dog has been healthy and exercised regularly throughout life, he may not slow down much at all. Only by paying attention to your dog's behavior and physical symptoms can you best monitor what he can and can't do and how much extra help he needs.

Some dogs can be revitalized by the introduction of a new puppy into the home, and other dogs may react against an overzealous intruder. Only you can judge if your dog would enjoy the company of a younger dog or if a puppy's constant quest for play would be more irritating than stimulating for your senior. If you do introduce a new puppy to the home, don't forget to give your senior dog the seniority he deserves, along with plenty of attention, love, and reassurance so that he doesn't feel he is being replaced but instead feels he is gaining a non-threatening buddy.

No matter how good or bad your senior dog is feeling, don't forget to continue spending quality time together so your dog knows he is loved and is able to enjoy his final years in your close company. That's what he really wants.

Saying Good-Bye

The hardest part of loving a dog must surely be when you have to say good-bye. Whether your dog succumbs to old age on her own or whether you make the decision to put an end to her pain and suffering when her quality of life is no longer tolerable, saying good-bye to a pet is a heart-wrenching experience.

If your aging pet is suffering pain that can't be remedied and if she has declined to the point that she no longer enjoys life, you may feel it is your responsibility as her guardian to put an end to her

Don't Redecorate

If your dog is losing his sight, make an effort to keep furniture in the same place. This isn't the time to redecorate the living room. Your vision-impaired dog is familiar with a certain layout to the house and moving things around can confuse and scare her.

Adding another dog to the household may lift your older dog's spirits.

Part 3

The experiences you share with your dog will make a lifetime of memories.

Your Dog Is Worth It!

Please remember that when you brought a dog into your life, you did so knowing you were committed to providing her with proper health care. Now that your dog is older and needs health care and your love and affection more than ever, please don't abandon her because she has become "too expensive" or "too much trouble." Remember all she has given you throughout her life, and consider what you can give her in return.

suffering. The decision to euthanize your pet is a difficult one—one of the most difficult decisions you may ever make. But if you grant your pet the ultimate kindness of ending her suffering, don't feel guilty. You have done the right thing.

And if you aren't sure? If your pet is debilitated but can still enjoy her life, then you may decide to let nature take its course. Talk to your vet, who may be able to give you advice. Your vet can determine, when you may not be able to, how much pain your dog is feeling, and can also help you to understand your dog's prospects for recovery and pain relief.

Whatever you and your vet decide, losing a beloved pet isn't easy. People often take many days, months, even years to stop feeling sad. You may become depressed or cry a lot. It's completely natural. Many books and websites are devoted to counseling and supporting those who have lost a pet. Gone are the days when those grieving over the loss of a pet feel silly for their sadness. Pets have become valued family members, and so many have lost pets that people understand. Seek support for your grief.

In the end, though dogs may not live as long as humans, the relationships we form with them and the love and affection we share make the dog-human relationship something beautiful and special. If you have done your part to give your dog a happy life with good health care, training, and lots of time together, you have given your dog the best possible life he could have. He has enriched your life, too. People all over the world who have loved and lost their pets agree: Loving and caring for a dog is worth every moment.

Organizations

American Dog Owner's Association, Inc

1654 Columbia Turnpike

Castleton, NY 12033

Website: www.adoa.org/

American Holistic Veterinary Medical Association

2218 Old Emmorton Road

Bel Air, MD 21015

Phone: 410-569-0795

Fax: 410-569-2346

Email: office@ahvma.org

American Kennel Club Canine Health Foundation

251 W. Garfield Road, Suite 160

Aurora, OH 44202-8856

Phone: 888-682-9696

Email: akcchf@aol.com

Website: www.akcchf.org

American Veterinary Medical Association

1931 North Meacham Road

Suite 100

Schaumburg, IL 60173

Phone: 847-925-8070

Fax: 847-925-1329

Email: avmainfo@avma.org

Association of Pet Dog Trainers

17000 Commerce Parkway

Suite C

Mt. Laurel, NJ 08054

Phone: 800-PET-DOGS

Website: www.apdt.com

Canine Eye Registration Foundation

Department of Veterinary Clinical Science

School of Veterinary Medicine

Perdue University

West Lafayette, IN 47907

Phone: 317-494-8179

Fax: 317-494-9981

Website: www.prodogs.com

Morris Animal Foundation

45 Inverness Drive East

Englewood, CO 80112-5480

Phone: 800-243-2345 or 303-790-2345

Website: www.morrisanimalfoundation.org

National Animal Poison Control Center

Phone: 888-426-4435 (you will be charged a $45 consultation fee to talk with a vet about

your pet's emergency)

Website: www.aspca.org

Orthopedic Foundation for Animals (OFA)

2300 E. Nifong Boulevard

Columbia, MO 65201-3856

Phone: 573-442-0418

Fax: 573-875-5073

Email: ofa@offa.org

Website: www.offa.org/

Wolves-n-Wildlife

2550 South Mountain Road

Fillmore, CA 93015

Phone: 805-524-0781

Email: info@wolvesnwildlife.com

Website: www.wolvesnwildlife.org/

Websites

Canine Health Problems by Breed
www.dogpack.com/health/healthproblems.htm

Canine Intervertebral Disk Disease
A publication of the Dachshund Club of America
www.dachshund-dca.org/diskbook.html.

Cindy Tittle Moore's Canine Medical Information FAQ:
www.faqs.org/faqs/dogs-faq/medical-info/part1/;
www.faqs.org/faqs/dogs-faq/medical-info/part2/

Dog Owner's Guide
www.canismajor.com/dog/index.html

Dog Watch
http://www.dogwatch.net/

Dogs Pet Health Care Library
www.pethealthcare.net/html/pet_care_library.html

Clicker Training
www.clickandtreat.com

How Dogs Think: A Non-Verbal Link to Canine Communication
www.webtrail.com/petbehavior/dogthink.html

Books

Coppinger, Raymond and Lorna Coppinger. *Dogs: A Startling New Understanding of Canine Origin, Behavior & Evolution.* New York: Scribner, 2001.

Giffin, James M., M.D., and Lisa D. Carlson, CVM. *Dog Owner's Home Veterinary Handbook, all new 3rd edition.* New York: Howell Book House, 2000.

Kennedy, Stacy. *The Simple Guide to Puppies.* Neptune City, NJ: TFH, 2000.

Masson, Jeffrey Moussaieff. *Dogs Never Lie About Love.* New York: Three Rivers Press, 1997.

Pitcairn, Richard H., DVM, Ph.D. and Susan Hubble Pitcairn. *Dr. Pitcairn's Complete Guide to Natural Health for Dogs & Cats.* Emmaus, Pennsylvania: Rodale Press, Inc., 1995.

The Complete Dog Book, Official Publication of the American Kennel Club, 19th revised edition. New York: John Wiley & Sons, 1997.

Volhard, Wendy and Kerry Brown, DVM. *Holistic Guide for a Healthy Dog, 2nd edition.* Foster City, CA: Howell Book House, 2000.

Walkowicz, Chris and Bonnie Wilcox, DVM. *Successful Dog Breeding, 2nd edition.* New York: Howell Book House, 1994.

William E. Campbell. *The New Better Behavior in Dogs.* Loveland, Colorado: Alpine Publications, 1999.

Index

Photo Credits